Thoughts on R

George John Romanes

(Editor: Charles Gore)

Alpha Editions

This edition published in 2023

ISBN : 9789357947893

Design and Setting By
Alpha Editions
www.alphaedis.com
Email - info@alphaedis.com

EDITOR'S PREFACE

The late Mr. George John Romanes—the author within the last few years of *Darwin and After Darwin*, and of the *Examination of Weismannism*—occupied a distinguished place in contemporary biology. But his mind was also continuously and increasingly active on the problems of metaphysics and theology. And at his death in the early summer of this year (1894), he left among his papers some notes, made mostly in the previous winter, for a work which he was intending to write on the fundamental questions of religion. He had desired that these notes should be given to me and that I should do with them as I thought best. His literary executors accordingly handed them over to me, in company with some unpublished essays, two of which form the first part of the present volume.

After reading the notes myself, and obtaining the judgement of others in whom I feel confidence upon them, I have no hesitation either in publishing by far the greater part of them, or in publishing them with the author's name in spite of the fact that the book as originally projected was to have been anonymous. From the few words which George Romanes said to me on the subject, I have no doubt that he realized that the notes if published after his death must be published with his name.

I have said that after reading these notes I feel no doubt that they ought to be published. They claim it both by their intrinsic value and by the light they throw on the religious thought of a scientific man who was not only remarkably able and clear-headed, but also many-sided, as few men are, in his capacities, and singularly candid and open-hearted. To all these qualities the notes which are now offered to the public will bear unmistakeable witness.

With more hesitation it has been decided to print also the unpublished essays already referred to. These, as representing an earlier stage of thought than is represented in the notes, naturally appear first.

Both Essays and Notes however represent the same tendency of a mind from a position of unbelief in the Christian Revelation toward one of belief in it. They represent, I say, a tendency of one 'seeking after God if haply he might feel after Him and find Him,' and not a position of settled orthodoxy. Even the Notes contain in fact many things which could not come from a settled believer. This being so it is natural that I should say a word as to the way in which I have understood my function as an editor. I have decided the question of publishing each Note solely by the consideration whether or no it was sufficiently finished to be intelligible. I have rigidly excluded any question of my own agreement or disagreement with it. In the case of one

Note in particular, I doubt whether I should have published it, had it not been that my decided disagreement with its contents made me fear that I might be prejudiced in withholding it.

The Notes, with the papers which precede them, will, I think, be better understood if I give some preliminary account of their antecedents, that is of Romanes' previous publications on the subject of religion.

In 1873 an essay of George Romanes gained the Burney Prize at Cambridge, the subject being *Christian Prayer considered in relation to the belief that the Almighty governs the world by general laws.* This was published in 1874, with an appendix on *The Physical Efficacy of Prayer.* In this essay, written when he was twenty-five years old, Romanes shows the characteristic qualities of his mind and style already developed. The sympathy with the scientific point of view is there, as might be expected perhaps in a Cambridge 'Scholar in Natural Science': the logical acumen and love of exact distinctions is there: there too the natural piety and spiritual appreciation of the nature of Christian prayer—a piety and appreciation which later intellectual habits of thought could never eradicate. The essay, as judged by the standard of prize compositions, is of remarkable ability, and strictly proceeds within the limits of the thesis. On the one side, for the purpose of the argument, the existence of a Personal God is assumed[1], and also the reality of the Christian Revelation which assures us that we have reason to expect real answers, even though conditionally and within restricted limits, to prayers for *physical* goods[2]. On the other side, there is taken for granted the belief that general laws pervade the observable domain of physical nature. Then the question is considered—how is the physical efficacy of prayer which the Christian accepts on the authority of revelation compatible with the scientifically known fact that God governs the world by general laws? The answer is mainly found in emphasizing the limited sphere within which scientific inquiry can be conducted and scientific knowledge can obtain. Special divine acts of response to prayer, even in the physical sphere, *may* occur—force *may* be even originated in response to prayer—and still not produce any phenomenon such as science must take cognizance of and regard as miraculous or contrary to the known order.

On one occasion the Notes refer back to this essay[3], and more frequently, as we shall have occasion to notice, they reproduce thoughts which had already been expressed in the earlier work but had been obscured or repudiated in the interval. I have no grounds for knowing whether in the main Romanes remained satisfied with the reasoning and conclusion of his earliest essay, granted the theistic hypothesis on which it rests[4]. But this hypothesis itself, very shortly after publishing this essay, he was led to repudiate. In other words, his mind moved rapidly and sharply into a position of reasoned scepticism about the existence of God at all. The Burney Essay was published in 1874. Already in 1876 at least he had written an anonymous work with a wholly sceptical conclusion, entitled 'A Candid Examination of Theism' by *Physicus*[5]. As the Notes were written with direct reference to this work, some detailed account of its argument seems necessary; and this is to be found in the last chapter of the work itself, where the author summarizes his arguments and draws his conclusions. I venture therefore to reproduce this chapter at length[6].

'§ 1. Our analysis is now at an end, and a very few words will here suffice to convey an epitomized recollection of the numerous facts and conclusions which we have found it necessary to contemplate. We first disposed of the conspicuously absurd supposition that the origin of things, or the mystery of existence [i.e. the fact that anything exists at all], admits of being explained by the theory of Theism in any further degree than by the theory of Atheism. Next it was shown that the argument "Our heart requires a God" is invalid, seeing that such a subjective necessity, even if made out, could not be sufficient to prove—or even to render probable—an objective existence. And with regard to the further argument that the fact of our theistic aspirations points to God as to their explanatory cause, it became necessary to observe that the argument could only be admissible after the possibility of the operation of natural causes [in the production of our theistic aspirations] had been excluded. Similarly the argument from the supposed intuitive necessity of individual thought [i.e. the alleged fact that men find it impossible to rid themselves of the persuasion that God exists] was found to be untenable, first, because, even if the supposed necessity were a real one, it would only possess an individual applicability; and second, that, as a matter of fact, it is extremely improbable that the supposed necessity is a real necessity even for the individual who asserts it, while it is absolutely certain that it is not such to the vast majority of the race. The argument from the general consent of mankind, being so obviously fallacious both as to facts and principles, was passed over without comment; while the argument from a first cause was found to involve a logical suicide. Lastly, the argument that, as human volition is a cause in nature, therefore all causation is probably volitional in character, was shown to consist in a stretch of inference so outrageous that the argument had to be pronounced worthless.

'§ 2. Proceeding next to examine the less superficial arguments in favour of Theism, it was first shown that the syllogism, All known minds are caused by an unknown mind; our mind is a known mind; therefore our mind is caused by an unknown mind,—is a syllogism that is inadmissible for two reasons. In the first place, it does not account for mind (in the abstract) to refer it to a prior mind for its origin; and therefore, although the hypothesis, if admitted, would be *an* explanation of *known* mind, it is useless as an argument for the existence of the unknown mind, the assumption of which forms the basis of that explanation. Again, in the next place, if it be said that mind is so far an entity *sui generis* that it must be either self-existing or caused by another mind, there is no assignable warrant for the assertion. And this is the second objection to the above syllogism; for anything within the whole range of the possible may, for aught that we can tell, be competent to produce a self-conscious intelligence. Thus an objector to the above syllogism need not hold any theory of things at all; but even as opposed to the definite theory of materialism, the above syllogism has not so valid an argumentative basis to stand upon. We know that what we call matter and force are to all appearance eternal, while we have no corresponding evidence of a mind that is even apparently eternal. Further, within experience mind is invariably associated with highly differentiated collocations of matter and distributions of force, and many facts go to prove, and none to negative, the conclusion that the grade of intelligence invariably depends upon, or at least is associated with, a corresponding grade of cerebral development. There is thus both a qualitative and a quantitative relation between intelligence and cerebral organisation. And if it is said that matter and motion cannot produce consciousness because it is inconceivable that they should, we have seen at some length that this is no conclusive consideration as applied to a subject of a confessedly transcendental nature, and that in the present case it is particularly inconclusive, because, as it is speculatively certain that the substance of mind must be unknowable, it seems *à priori* probable that, whatever is the cause of the unknowable reality, this cause should be more difficult to render into thought in that relation than would some other hypothetical substance which is imagined as more akin to mind. And if it is said that the *more* conceivable cause is the *more* probable cause, we have seen that it is in this case impossible to estimate the validity of the remark. Lastly, the statement that the cause must contain actually all that its effects can contain, was seen to be inadmissible in logic and contradicted by everyday experience; while the argument from the supposed freedom of the will and the existence of the moral sense was negatived both deductively by the theory of evolution, and inductively by the doctrine of utilitarianism.' The theory of the freedom of the will is indeed at this stage of thought utterly untenable[7]; the evidence is overwhelming that the moral sense is the result of a purely natural evolution[8], and this result, arrived at on general grounds, is confirmed with irresistible force by the account of our human conscience which is supplied by the theory of utilitarianism, a theory based on the widest and most unexceptionable of inductions[9]. 'On the whole, then, with regard to the argument from the existence of the human mind, we were compelled to decide that it is destitute of any assignable weight, there being nothing more to lead to the conclusion that our mind has been caused by another mind, than to the conclusion that it has been caused by anything else whatsoever.

'§ 3. With regard to the argument from Design, it was observed that Mill's presentation of it [in his *Essay on Theism*] is merely a resuscitation of the argument as presented by Paley, Bell, and Chalmers. And indeed we saw that the first-named writer treated this whole subject with a feebleness and inaccuracy very surprising in him; for while he has failed to assign anything like due weight to the inductive evidence of organic evolution, he did not hesitate to rush into a supernatural explanation of biological phenomena. Moreover, he has failed signally in his *analysis* of the Design argument, seeing that, in common with all previous writers, he failed to observe that it is utterly impossible for us to know the relations in which the supposed Designer stands to the Designed,—much less to argue from the fact that the Supreme Mind, even supposing it to exist, caused the observable products by any particular intellectual *process*. In other words, all advocates of the Design argument have failed to perceive that, even if we grant nature to be due to a creating Mind, still we have no shadow of a right to conclude that this Mind can only have exerted its creative power by means of such and such cogitative operations. How absurd, therefore, must it be to raise the supposed evidence of such cogitative operations into evidences of the existence of a creating Mind! If a theist retorts that it is, after all, of very little importance whether or not we are able to divine the *methods* of creation, so long as the *facts* are there to attest that, *in some way or other*, the observable phenomena of nature must be due to Intelligence of some kind as their ultimate cause, then I am the first to endorse this remark. It has always appeared to me one of the most unaccountable things in the history of speculation that so many competent writers can have insisted upon *Design* as an argument for Theism, when they must all have known perfectly well that they have no means of ascertaining the subjective psychology of that Supreme Mind whose existence the argument is adduced to demonstrate. The truth is, that the argument from teleology must, and can only, rest upon the observable *facts* of nature, without reference to the intellectual *processes* by which these facts may be supposed to have been accomplished. But, looking to the "present state of our knowledge," this is merely to change the teleological argument in its gross Paleyian form, into the argument from the ubiquitous operation of general laws.'

'§ 4. This argument was thus[10] stated in contrast with the argument from design. 'The argument from design says, there must be a God, because such and such an organic structure must have been due to such and such an intellectual *process*. The argument from general laws says, There must be a God, because such and such an organic structure must *in some way or other have been ultimately due to* intelligence.' Every structure exhibits with more or less of complexity the principle of order; it is related to all other things in a universal order. This universality of order renders irrational the hypothesis of chance in accounting for the universe. 'Let us think of the supreme causality as we may, the fact remains that from it there emanates a directive influence of uninterrupted consistency, on a scale of stupendous magnitude and exact precision worthy of our highest conceptions of deity[11].' The argument was developed in the words of Professor Baden Powell. 'That which requires reason and thought to understand must be itself thought and reason. That which mind alone can investigate or express must be itself mind. And if the highest conception attained is but partial, then the mind and reason studied is greater than the mind and reason of the student. If the more it is studied the more vast and complex is the necessary connection in reason disclosed, then the more evident is the vast extent and compass of the reason thus partially manifested and its reality *as existing in the immutably connected order of objects examined,* independently of the mind of the investigator.' This argument from the universal *Kosmos* has the advantage of being wholly independent of the method by which things came to be what they are. It is unaffected by the acceptance of evolution. Till quite recently it seemed irrefutable[12].

'But nevertheless we are constrained to acknowledge that its apparent power dwindles to nothing in view of the indisputable fact that, if force and matter have been eternal, all and every natural law must have resulted by way of necessary consequence.... It does not admit of one moment's questioning that it is as certainly true that all the exquisite beauty and melodious harmony of nature follows necessarily as inevitably from the persistence of force and the primary qualities of matter as it is certainly true that force is persistent or that matter is extended or impenetrable[13].... It will be remembered that I dwelt at considerable length and with much earnestness upon this truth, not only because of its enormous importance in its bearing upon our subject, but also because no one has hitherto considered it in that relation.' It was also pointed out that the coherence and correspondence of the macrocosm of the universe with the microcosm of the human mind can be accounted for by the fact that the human mind is only one of the products of general evolution, its subjective relations necessarily reflecting those external relations of which they themselves are the product[14].

'§ 5. The next step, however, was to mitigate the severity of the conclusion that was liable to be formed upon the utter and hopeless collapse of all the possible arguments in favour of Theism. Having fully demonstrated that there is no shadow of a positive argument in support of the theistic theory, there arose the danger that some persons might erroneously conclude that for this reason the theistic theory must be untrue. It therefore became necessary to point out, that although, as far as we can see, nature does not require an Intelligent Cause to account for any of her phenomena, yet it is possible that, if we could see farther, we should see that nature could not be what she is unless she had owed her existence to an Intelligent Cause. Or, in other words, the probability there is that an Intelligent Cause is unnecessary to explain any of the phenomena of nature, is only equal to the probability there is that the doctrine of the persistence of force is everywhere and eternally true.

'As a final step in our analysis, therefore, we altogether quitted the region of experience, and ignoring even the very foundations of science, and so all the most certain of relative truths, we carried the discussion into the transcendental region of purely formal considerations. And here we laid down the canon, "that the value of any probability, in its last analysis, is determined by the number, the importance, and the definiteness of the relations known, as compared with those of the relations unknown;" and, consequently, that in cases where the unknown relations are more numerous, more important, or more indefinite than are the known relations, the value of our inference varies inversely as the difference in these respects between the relations compared. From which canon it followed, that as the problem of Theism is the most ultimate of all problems, and so contains in its unknown relations all that is to man unknown and unknowable, these relations must be pronounced the most indefinite of all relations that it is possible for man to contemplate; and, consequently, that although we have here the entire range of experience from which to argue, we are unable to estimate the real value of any argument whatsoever. The unknown relations in our attempted induction being wholly indefinite, both in respect of their number and importance, as compared with the known relations, it is impossible for us to determine any definite probability either for or against the being of a God. Therefore, although it is true that, so far as human science can penetrate or human thought infer, we can perceive no evidence of God, yet we have no right on this account to conclude that there is no God. The probability, therefore, that nature is devoid of Deity, while it is of the strongest kind if regarded scientifically—amounting, in fact, to a scientific demonstration,—is nevertheless wholly worthless if regarded logically. Although it is as true as is the fundamental basis of all science and of all experience that, if there is a God, His existence, considered as a cause of the universe, is superfluous, it may nevertheless be true that, if there had never been a God, the universe could never have existed.

'Hence these formal considerations proved conclusively that, no matter how great the probability of Atheism might appear to be in a relative sense, we have no means of estimating such probability in an absolute sense. From which position there emerged the possibility of another argument in favour of Theism—or rather let us say, of a reappearance of the teleological argument in another form. For it may be said, seeing that these formal considerations exclude legitimate reasoning either for or against Deity in an absolute sense, while they do not exclude such reasoning in a relative sense, if there yet remain any theistic deductions which may properly be drawn from experience, these may now be adduced to balance the atheistic deductions from the persistence of force. For although the latter deductions have clearly shown the existence of Deity to be superfluous in a scientific sense, the formal considerations in question have no less clearly opened up beyond the sphere of science a possible *locus* for the existence of Deity; so that if there are any facts supplied by experience for which the atheistic deductions appear insufficient to account, we are still free to account for them in a relative sense by the hypothesis of Theism. And, it may be urged, we do find such an unexplained residuum in the correlation of general laws in the production of cosmic harmony. It signifies nothing, the argument may run, that we are unable to conceive the methods whereby the supposed Mind operates in producing cosmic harmony; nor does it signify that its operation must now be relegated to a super-scientific province. What does signify is that, taking a general view of nature, we find it impossible to conceive of the extent and variety of her harmonious processes as other than products of intelligent causation. Now this sublimated form of the teleological argument, it will be remembered, I denoted a metaphysical teleology, in order sharply to distinguish it from all previous forms of that argument, which, in contradistinction I denoted scientific teleologies. And the distinction, it will be remembered, consisted in this—that while all previous forms of teleology, by resting on a basis which was not beyond the possible reach of science, laid themselves open to the possibility of scientific refutation, the metaphysical system of teleology, by resting on a basis which is clearly beyond the possible reach of science, can never be susceptible of scientific refutation. And that this metaphysical system of teleology does rest on such a basis is indisputable; for while it accepts the most ultimate truths of which science can ever be cognizant—viz. the persistence of force and the consequently necessary genesis of natural law,—it nevertheless maintains that the necessity of regarding Mind as the ultimate cause of things is not on this account removed; and, therefore, that if science now requires the operation of a Supreme Mind to be posited in a super-scientific sphere, then in a super-scientific sphere it ought to be posited. No doubt this hypothesis at first sight seems gratuitous, seeing that, so far as science can penetrate, there is no need of any such hypothesis at all—cosmic harmony resulting as a physically necessary consequence from the combined action of natural laws, which in turn result as a physically necessary consequence of the persistence of force and the primary qualities of matter. But although it is thus indisputably true that metaphysical teleology is wholly gratuitous if considered scientifically, it may not be true that it is wholly gratuitous if considered psychologically. In other words, if it is more conceivable that Mind should be the ultimate cause of cosmic harmony than that the persistence of force should be so, then it is not irrational to accept the more conceivable hypothesis in preference to the less conceivable one, provided that the choice is made with the diffidence which is required by the considerations adduced in Chapter V [especially the *Canon of probability* laid down in the second paragraph of this section, § 5].

'I conclude, therefore, that the hypothesis of metaphysical teleology, although in a physical sense gratuitous, may be in a psychological sense legitimate. But as against the fundamental position on which alone this argument can rest—viz. the position that the fundamental postulate of Atheism is more *inconceivable* than is the fundamental postulate of Theism—we have seen two important objections to lie.

'For, in the first place, the sense in which the word "inconceivable" is here used is that of the impossibility of framing *realizable* relations in the thought; not that of the impossibility of framing *abstract* relations in thought. In the same sense, though in a lower degree, it is true that the complexity of the human organization and its functions is inconceivable; but in this sense the word "inconceivable" has much less weight in an argument than it has in its true sense. And, without waiting again to dispute (as we did in the case of the speculative standing of Materialism) how far even the genuine test of inconceivability ought to be allowed to make against an inference which there is a body of scientific evidence to substantiate, we went on to the second objection against this fundamental position of metaphysical teleology. This objection, it will be remembered, was, that it is as impossible to conceive of cosmic harmony as an effect of Mind [i.e. Mind being what we know it in experience to be], as it is to conceive of it as an effect of mindless evolution. The argument from inconceivability, therefore, admits of being turned with quite as terrible an effect on Theism, as it can possibly be made to exert on Atheism.

'Hence this more refined form of teleology which we are considering, and which we saw to be the last of the possible arguments in favour of Theism, is met on its own ground by a very crushing opposition: by its metaphysical character it has escaped the opposition of physical science, only to encounter a new opposition in the region of pure psychology to which it fled. As a conclusion to our whole inquiry, therefore, it devolved on us to determine the relative magnitudes of these opposing forces. And in doing this we first observed that, if the supporters of metaphysical teleology objected *à priori* to the method whereby the genesis of natural law was deduced from the datum of the persistence of force, in that this method involved an unrestricted use of illegitimate symbolic conceptions; then it is no less open to an atheist to object *à priori* to the method whereby a directing Mind was inferred from the datum of cosmic harmony, in that this method involved the postulation of an unknowable cause,—and this of a character which the whole history of human thought has proved the human mind to exhibit an overweening tendency to postulate as the cause of natural phenomena. On these grounds, therefore, I concluded that, so far as their respective standing *à priori* is concerned, both theories may be regarded as about equally suspicious. And similarly with regard to their standing *à posteriori*; for as both theories require to embody at least one infinite term, they must each alike be pronounced absolutely inconceivable. But, finally, if the question were put to me which of the two theories I regarded as the more rational, I observed that this is a question which no one man can answer for another. For as the test of absolute inconceivability is equally destructive of both theories, if a man wishes to choose between them, his choice can only be determined by what I have designated relative inconceivability—i.e. in accordance with the verdict given by his individual sense of probability as determined by his previous habit of thought. And forasmuch as the test of relative inconceivability may be held in this matter legitimately to vary with the character of the mind which applies it, the strictly rational probability of the question to which it is applied varies in like manner. Or otherwise presented, the only alternative for any man in this matter is either to discipline himself into an attitude of pure scepticism, and thus to refuse in thought to entertain either a probability or an improbability concerning the existence of a God; or else to incline in thought towards an affirmation or a negation of God, according as his previous habits of thought have rendered such an inclination more facile in the one direction than in the other. And although, under such circumstances, I should consider that man the more rational who carefully suspended his judgement, I conclude that if this course is departed from, neither the metaphysical teleologist nor the scientific atheist has any perceptible advantage over the other in respect of rationality. For as the formal conditions of a metaphysical teleology are undoubtedly present on the one hand, and the formal conditions of a speculative atheism are as undoubtedly present on the other, there is thus in both cases a logical vacuum supplied wherein the pendulum of thought is free to swing in whichever direction it may be made to swing by the momentum of preconceived ideas.

'§ 6. Such is the outcome of our investigation, and considering the abstract nature of the subject, the immense divergence of opinion which at the present time is manifested with regard to it, as well as the confusing amount of good, bad and indifferent literature on both sides of the controversy which is extant;—considering these things, I do not think that the result of our inquiry can be justly complained of on the score of its lacking precision. At a time like the present, when traditional beliefs respecting Theism are so generally accepted, and so commonly concluded as a matter of course to have a large and valid basis of induction whereon to rest, I cannot but feel that a perusal of this short essay, by showing how very concise the scientific *status* of the subject really is, will do more to settle the minds of most readers as to the exact standing at the present time of all the probabilities of the question, than could a perusal of all the rest of the literature upon this subject. And, looking to the present condition of speculative philosophy, I regard it as of the utmost importance to have clearly shown that the advance of science has now entitled us to assert, without the least hesitation, that the hypothesis of Mind in nature is as certainly superfluous to account for any of the phenomena of nature, as the scientific doctrine of the persistence of force and the indestructibility of matter is certainly true.

'On the other hand, if any one is inclined to complain that the logical aspect of the question has not proved itself so unequivocally definite as has the scientific, I must ask him to consider that, in any matter which does not admit of actual demonstration, some margin must of necessity be left for variations of individual opinion. And, if he bears this consideration in mind, I feel sure that he cannot properly complain of my not having done my utmost in this case to define as sharply as possible the character and the limits of this margin.

'§ 7. And now, in conclusion, I feel it is desirable to state that any antecedent bias with regard to Theism which I individually possess is unquestionably on the side of traditional beliefs. It is therefore with the utmost sorrow that I find myself compelled to accept the conclusions here worked out; and nothing would have induced me to publish them, save the strength of my conviction that it is the duty of every member of society to give his fellows the benefit of his labours for whatever they may be worth. Just as I am confident that truth must in the end be the most profitable for the race, so I am persuaded that every individual endeavour to attain it, provided only that such endeavour is unbiassed and sincere, ought without hesitation to be made the common property of all men, no matter in what direction the results of its promulgation may appear to tend. And so far as the ruination of individual happiness is concerned, no one can have a more lively perception than myself of the possibly disastrous tendency of my work. So far as I am individually concerned, the result of this analysis has been to show that, whether I regard the problem of Theism on the lower plane of strictly relative probability, or on the higher plane of purely formal considerations, it equally becomes my obvious duty to stifle all belief of the kind which I conceive to be the noblest, and to discipline my intellect with regard to this matter into an attitude of the purest scepticism. And forasmuch as I am far from being able to agree with those who affirm that the twilight doctrine of the "new faith" is a desirable substitute for the waning splendour of "the old," I am not ashamed to confess that with this virtual negation of God the universe to me has lost its soul of loveliness; and although from henceforth the precept to "work while it is day" will doubtless but gain an intensified force from the terribly intensified meaning of the words that "the night cometh when no man can work," yet when at times I think, as think at times I must, of the appalling contrast between the hallowed glory of that creed which once was mine, and the lonely mystery of existence as now I find it,—

at such times I shall ever feel it impossible to avoid the sharpest pang of which my nature is susceptible. For whether it be due to my intelligence not being sufficiently advanced to meet the requirements of the age, or whether it be due to the memory of those sacred associations which to me at least were the sweetest that life has given, I cannot but feel that for me, and for others who think as I do, there is a dreadful truth in those words of Hamilton,—Philosophy having become a meditation, not merely of death, but of annihilation, the precept *know thyself* has become transformed into the terrific oracle to Œdipus—

> "Mayest thou ne'er know the truth of what thou art."'

This analysis will have been at least sufficient to give a clear idea of the general argument of the *Candid Examination* and of its melancholy conclusions. What will most strike a somewhat critical reader is perhaps (1) the tone of certainty, and (2) the belief in the almost exclusive right of the scientific method in the court of reason.

As evidence of (1) I would adduce the following brief quotations:—

> P. xi. 'Possible errors in reasoning apart, the rational position of Theism as here defined must remain without material modification as long as our intelligence remains human.'

> P. 24. 'I am quite unable to understand how any one at the present day, and with the most moderate powers of abstract thinking, can possibly bring himself to embrace the theory of Free-will.'

> P. 64. 'Undoubtedly we have no alternative but to conclude that the hypothesis of mind in nature is now logically proved to be as certainly superfluous as the very basis of all science is certainly true. There can no longer be any more doubt that the existence of a God is wholly unnecessary to explain any of the phenomena of the universe, than there is doubt that if I leave go of my pen it will fall upon the table.'

As evidence of (2) I would adduce from the preface—

> 'To my mind, therefore, it is impossible to resist the conclusion that, looking to this undoubted pre-eminence of the scientific methods as ways to truth, whether or not there is a God, the question as to his existence is both more morally and more reverently contemplated if we regard it purely as a problem for methodical analysis to solve, than if we regard it in any other light.'

It is in respect both of (1) and (2) that the change in Romanes' thought as exhibited in his later Notes is most conspicuous[15].

At what date George Romanes' mind began to react from the conclusions of the *Candid Examination* I cannot say. But after a period of ten years—in his Rede lecture of 1885[16]—we find his frame of mind very much changed. This lecture, on *Mind and Motion*, consists of a severe criticism of the materialistic account of mind. On the other hand 'spiritualism'—or the theory which would suppose that mind is the cause of motion—is pronounced from the point of view of science not impossible indeed but 'unsatisfactory,' and the more probable conclusion is found in a 'monism' like Bruno's—according to which mind and motion are co-ordinate and probably co-extensive aspects of the same universal fact—a monism which may be called Pantheism, but may also be regarded as an extension of contracted views of Theism[17]. The position represented by this lecture may be seen sufficiently from its conclusion:—

'If the advance of natural science is now steadily leading us to the conclusion that there is no motion without mind, must we not see how the independent conclusion of mental science is thus independently confirmed—the conclusion, I mean, that there is no being without knowing? To me, at least, it does appear that the time has come when we may begin, as it were in a dawning light, to see that the study of Nature and the study of Mind are meeting upon this greatest of possible truths. And if this is the case—if there is no motion without mind, no being without knowing—shall we infer, with Clifford, that universal being is mindless, or answer with a dogmatic negative that most stupendous of questions,—Is there knowledge with the Most High? If there is no motion without mind, no being without knowing, may we not rather infer, with Bruno, that it is in the medium of mind, and in the medium of knowledge, we live, and move, and have our being?

'This, I think, is the direction in which the inference points, if we are careful to set out the logical conditions with complete impartiality. But the ulterior question remains, whether, so far as science is concerned, it is here possible to point any inference at all: the whole orbit of human knowledge may be too narrow to afford a parallax for measurements so vast. Yet even here, if it be true that the voice of science must thus of necessity speak the language of agnosticism, at least let us see to it that the language is pure[18]; let us not tolerate any barbarisms introduced from the side of aggressive dogma. So shall we find that this new grammar of thought does not admit of any constructions radically opposed to more venerable ways of thinking; even if we do not find that the often-quoted words of its earliest formulator apply with special force to its latest dialects—that if a little knowledge of physiology and a little knowledge of psychology dispose men to atheism, a deeper knowledge of both, and, still more, a deeper thought upon their relations to one another, will lead men back to some form of religion, which if it be more vague, may also be more worthy than that of earlier days.'

Some time before 1889 three articles were written for the *Nineteenth Century* on the *Influence of Science upon Religion.* They were never published, for what reason I am not able to ascertain. But I have thought it worth while to print the first two of them as a 'first part' of this volume, both because they contain—written in George Romanes' own name—an important criticism upon the *Candid Examination* which he had published anonymously, and also because, with their entirely sceptical result, they exhibit very clearly a stage in the mental history of their author. The antecedents of these papers those who have read this Introduction will now be in a position to understand. What remains to be said by way of further introduction to the Notes had better be reserved till later.

C.G.

FOOTNOTES:

[1] p. 7.

[2] p. 173.

[3] See p. 110.

[4] But see an interesting note in Romanes' *Mind and Motion and Monism* (Longmans, 1895) p. 111.

[5] Published in Trübner's *English and Foreign Philosophical Library* in 1878, but written 'several years ago' (preface). 'I have refrained from publishing it,' the author explains, 'lest, after having done so, I should find that more mature thought had modified the conclusions which the author sets forth.'

[6] At times I have sought to make the argument of the chapter more intelligible by introducing references to earlier parts of the book or explanations in my own words. These latter I have inserted in square brackets.

[7] p. 24.

[8] p. 28.

[9] p. 28.

[10] p. 45.

[11] p. 47.

[12] p. 50.

[13] p. 63.

[14] pp. 58 ff.

[15] With reference to the views and arguments of the *Candid Examination*, it may be interesting to notice here in detail that George Romanes (1) came to attach much more importance to the subjective religious needs and intuitions of the human spirit (pp. 131 ff.); (2) perceived that the subjective religious consciousness can be regarded objectively as a broad human phenomenon (pp. 147 f.); (3) criticized his earlier theory of causation and returned *towards* the theory that all causation is volitional (pp. 102, 118); (4) definitely repudiated the materialistic account of the origin of mind (pp. 30, 31); (5) returned to the use of the expression 'the argument from design,' and therefore presumably abandoned his strong objection to it; (6) 'saw through' Herbert Spencer's refutation of the wider teleology expressed by Baden Powell, and felt the force of the teleology again (p. 72); (7) recognized that the scientific objections to the doctrine of the freedom of the will are not finally valid (p. 128).

[16] See *Mind and Motion and Monism*, pp. 36 ff.

[17] In some 'Notes' of the Summer of 1893 I find the statement, 'The result (of philosophical inquiry) has been that in his millennial contemplation and experience man has attained certainty with regard to certain aspects of the world problem, no less secure than that which he has gained in the domain of physical science, e.g.

Logical priority of mind over matter.

Consequent untenability of materialism.

Relativity of knowledge.

The order of nature, conservation of energy and indestructibility of matter within human experience, the principle of evolution and survival of the fittest.'

[18] For the meaning of 'pure' agnosticism see below. ff.

PART I.

THE INFLUENCE OF SCIENCE UPON RELIGION.

I.

I propose to consider, in a series of three papers, the influence of Science upon Religion. In doing this I shall seek to confine myself to the strictly rational aspect of the subject, without travelling into any matters of sentiment. Moreover, I shall aim at estimating in the first instance the kind and degree of influence which has been exerted by Science upon Religion in the past, and then go on to estimate the probable extent of this influence in the future. The first two papers will be devoted to the past and prospective influence of Science upon Natural Religion, while the third will be devoted to the past and prospective influence of Science upon Revealed Religion[19].

Few subjects have excited so much interest of late years as that which I thus mark out for discussion. This can scarcely be considered a matter of surprise, seeing that the influence in question is not only very direct, but also extremely important from every point of view. For generations and for centuries in succession Religion maintained an undisputed sway over men's minds—if not always as a practical guide in matters of conduct, at least as a regulator of belief. Even among the comparatively few who in previous centuries professedly rejected Christianity, there can be no doubt that their intellectual conceptions were largely determined by it: for Christianity being then the only court of appeal with reference to all these conceptions, even the few minds which were professedly without its jurisdiction could scarcely escape its indirect influence through the minds of others. But as side by side with the venerable institution a new court of appeal was gradually formed, we cannot wonder that it should have come to be regarded in the light of a rival to the old—more especially as the searching methods of its inquiry and the certain character of its judgements were much more in consonance with the requirements of an age disposed to scepticism. And this spirit of rivalry is still further fostered by the fact that Science has unquestionably exerted upon Religion what Mr. Fiske terms a 'purifying influence.' That is to say, not only are the scientific methods of inquiry after truth more congenial to sceptical minds than are the religious methods (which may broadly be defined as accepting truth on authority), but the results of the former have more than once directly contradicted those of the latter: science has in several cases incontestably demonstrated that religious teaching has been wrong as to matters of fact. Further still, the great advance of natural knowledge which has characterized the present century, has caused our ideas upon many subjects connected with philosophy to undergo a complete metamorphosis. A well-educated man of the present day is absolutely precluded from regarding some of the Christian dogmas from the same intellectual standpoint as his forefathers, even though he may still continue to accept them in some other sense. In short, our whole key of thinking or tone of thought having been in certain respects changed, we can no longer anticipate that in these respects it should continue to harmonize with the unalterable system of theology.

Such I conceive to be the ways in which Science has exerted her influence upon Religion, and it is needless to dwell upon the potency of their united effect. No one can read even a newspaper without perceiving how great this effect has been. On the one hand, sceptics are triumphantly confident that the light of dawning knowledge has begun finally to dispel the darkness of superstition, while religious persons, on the other hand, tremble to think what the future, if judged by the past, is likely to bring forth. On both sides we have free discussion, strong language, and earnest canvassing. Year by year stock is taken, and year by year the balance is found to preponderate in favour of Science.

This being the state of things of the present time, I think that with the experience of the kind and degree of influence which Science has exerted upon Religion in the past, we have material enough whereby to estimate the probable extent of such influence in the future. This, therefore, I shall endeavour to do by seeking to define, on general principles, the limits within which it is antecedently possible that the influence in question can be exercised. But in order to do this, it is necessary to begin by estimating the kind and degree of the influence which has been exerted by Science upon Religion in the past.

Thus much premised, we have in the first place to define the essential nature both of Science and of Religion: for this is clearly the first step in an analysis which has for its object an estimation of the actual and possible effects of one of these departments of thought upon the other.

Science, then, is essentially a department of thought having exclusive reference to the Proximate. More particularly, it is a department of thought having for its object the explanation of natural phenomena by the discovery of natural (or proximate) causes. In so far as Science ventures to trespass beyond this her only legitimate domain, and seeks to interpret natural phenomena by the immediate agency of supernatural or ultimate causes, in that degree has she ceased to be physical science, and become ontological speculation. The truth of this statement has now been practically recognized by all scientific workers; and terms describing final causes have been banished from their vocabulary in astronomy, chemistry, geology, biology, and even in psychology.

Religion, on the other hand, is a department of thought having no less exclusive reference to the Ultimate. More particularly, it is a department of thought having for its object a self-conscious and intelligent Being, which it regards as a Personal God, and the fountain-head of all causation. I am, of course, aware that the term Religion has been of late years frequently used in senses which this definition would not cover; but I conceive that this only shows how frequently the term in question has been abused. To call any theory of things a Religion which does not present any belief in any form of Deity, is to apply the word to the very opposite of that which it has hitherto been used to denote. To speak of the Religion of the Unknowable, the Religion of Cosmism, the Religion of Humanity, and so forth, where the personality of the First Cause is not recognized, is as unmeaning as it would be to speak of the love of a triangle, or the rationality of the equator. That is to say, if any meaning is to be extracted from the terms at all, it is only to be so by using them in some metaphorical sense. We may, for instance, say that there is such a thing as a Religion of Humanity, because we may begin by deifying Humanity in our own estimation, and then go on to worship our ideal. But by thus giving Humanity the name of Deity we are not really creating a new religion: we are merely using a metaphor, which may or may not be successful as a matter of poetic diction, but which most assuredly presents no shred of value as a matter of philosophical statement. Indeed, in this relation it is worse than valueless: it is misleading. Variations or reversals in the meanings of words are not of uncommon occurrence in the ordinary growth of languages; but it is not often that we find, as in this case, the whole meaning of a term intentionally and gratuitously changed by the leaders of philosophical thought. Humanity, for example, is an abstract idea of our own making: it is not an object any more than the equator is an object. Therefore, if it were possible to construct a religion by this curious device of metaphorically ascribing to Humanity the attributes of Deity, it ought to be as logically possible to construct, let us say, a theory of brotherly regard towards the equator, by metaphorically ascribing to it the attributes of man. The distinguishing features of any theory which can properly be termed a Religion, is that it should refer to the ultimate source, or sources, of things: and that it should suppose this source to be of an objective, intelligent, and personal nature. To apply the term Religion to any other theory is merely to abuse it.

From these definitions, then, it appears that the aims and methods of Science are exclusively concerned with the ascertaining and the proof of the proximate How of things and processes physical: her problem is, as Mill states it, to discover what are the fewest number of (phenomenal) data which, being granted, will explain the phenomena of experience. On the other hand, Religion is not in any way concerned with causation, further than to assume that all things and all processes are ultimately due to intelligent personality. Religion is thus, as Mr. Spencer says, 'an *à priori* theory of the universe'—to which, however, we must add, 'and a theory which assumes intelligent personality as the originating source of the universe.' Without this needful addition, a religion would be in no way logically distinguished from a philosophy.

From these definitions, then, it clearly follows that in their purest forms, Science and Religion really have no point of logical contact. Only if Science could transcend the conditions of space and time, of phenomenal relativity, and of all human limitations, only then could Science be in a position to touch the supernatural theory of Religion. But obviously, if Science could do this, she would cease to be Science. In soaring above the region of phenomena and entering the tenuous aether of noumena, her present wings, which we call her methods, would in such an atmosphere be no longer of any service for movement. Out of time, out of place, and out of phenomenal relation, Science could no longer exist as such.

On the other hand, Religion in its purest form is equally incompetent to affect Science. For, as we have already seen, Religion as such is not concerned with the phenomenal sphere: her theory of ontology cannot have any reference to the How of phenomenal causation. Hence it is evident that, as in their purest or most ideal forms they move in different mental planes, Science and Religion cannot exhibit interference.

Thus far the remarks which I have made apply equally to all forms of Religion, as such, whether actual or possible, and in so far as the Religion is *pure*. But it is notorious that until quite recently Religion did exercise upon Science, not only an influence, but an overpowering influence. Belief in divine agency being all but universal, while the methods of scientific research had not as yet been distinctly formulated, it was in previous generations the usual habit of mind to refer any natural phenomenon, the physical causation of which had not been ascertained, to the more or less immediate causal action of the Deity. But we now see that this habit of mind arose from a failure to distinguish between the essentially distinct characters of Science and Religion as departments of thought, and therefore that it was only so far as the Religion of former times was impure—or mixed with the ingredients of thought which belong to Science—that the baleful influence in question was exerted. The gradual, successive, and now all but total abolition of final causes from the thoughts of scientific men, to which allusion has already been made, is merely an expression of the fact that scientific men as a body have come fully to recognize the fundamental distinction between Science and Religion which I have stated.

Or, to put the matter in another way, scientific men as a body—and, indeed, all persons whose ideas on such matters are abreast of the times—perceive plainly enough that a religious explanation of any natural phenomenon is, from a scientific point of view, no explanation at all. For a religious explanation consists in referring the observed phenomenon to the First

Cause—i.e. to merge that particular phenomenon in the general or final mystery of things. A scientific explanation, on the other hand, consists in referring the observed phenomenon to its physical causes, and in no case can such an explanation entertain the hypothesis of a final cause without abandoning its character as a scientific explanation. For example, if a child brings me a flower and asks why it has such a curious form, bright colour, sweet perfume, and so on, and if I answer, Because God made it so, I am not really answering the child's question: I am merely concealing my ignorance of Nature under a guise of piety, and excusing my indolence in the study of botany. It was the appreciation of this fact that led Mr. Darwin to observe in his *Origin of Species* that the theory of creation does not serve to explain any of the facts with which it is concerned, but merely re-states these facts as they are observed to occur. That is to say, by thus merging the facts as observed into the final mystery of things, we are not even attempting to explain them in any scientific sense: for it would be obviously possible to get rid of the necessity of thus explaining any natural phenomenon whatsoever by referring it to the immediate causal action of the Deity. If any phenomenon were actually to occur which did proceed from the immediate causal action of the Deity, then *ex hypothesi*, there would be no physical causes to investigate, and the occupation of Othello, in the person of a man of science, would be gone. Such a phenomenon would be miraculous, and therefore from its very nature beyond the reach of scientific investigation.

Properly speaking, then, the religious theory of final causes does not explain any of the phenomena of Nature: it merely re-states the phenomena as observed—or, if we prefer so to say, it is itself an ultimate and universal explanation of all possible phenomena taken collectively. For it must be admitted that behind all possible explanations of a scientific kind, there lies a great inexplicable, which just because of its ultimate character, cannot be merged into anything further—that is to say, cannot be explained. 'It is what it is,' is all that we can say of it: 'I am that I am' is all that it could say of itself. And it is in referring phenomena to this inexplicable source of physical causation that the theory of Religion essentially consists. The theory of Science, on the other hand, consists in the assumption that there is always a practically endless chain of physical causation to investigate—i.e. an endless series of phenomena to be explained. So that, if we define the process of explanation as the process of referring observed phenomena to their adequate causes, we may say that Religion, by the aid of a general theory of things in the postulation of an intelligent First Cause, furnishes to her own satisfaction an ultimate explanation of the universe as a whole, and therefore is not concerned with any of those proximate explanations or discovery of second causes, which form the exclusive subject-matter of Science. In other words, we recur to the definitions already stated, to the effect that Religion is a department of thought having, as such, exclusive reference to the

Ultimate, while Science is a department of thought having, as such, no less exclusive reference to the Proximate. When these two departments of thought overlap, interference results, and we find confusion. Therefore it was that when the religious theory of final causes intruded upon the field of scientific inquiry, it was passing beyond its logical domain; and seeking to arrogate the function of explaining this or that phenomenon *in detail*, it ceased to be a purely religious theory, while at the same time and for the same reason it blocked the way of scientific progress[20].

This remark serves to introduce one of the chief topics with which I have to deal—viz. the doctrine of Design in Nature, and thus the whole question of Natural Religion in its relation to Natural Science. In handling this topic I shall endeavour to take as broad and deep a view as I can of the present standing of Natural Religion, without waiting to show step by step the ways and means by which it has been brought into this position, by the influence of Science.

In the earliest dawn of recorded thought, teleology in some form or another has been the most generally accepted theory whereby the order of Nature is explained. It is not, however, my object in this paper to trace the history of this theory from its first rude beginnings in Fetishism to its final development in Theism. I intend to devote myself exclusively to the question as to the present standing of this theory, and I allude to its past history only in order to examine the statement which is frequently made, to the effect that its general prevalence in all ages and among all peoples of the world lends to it a certain degree of 'antecedent credibility.' With reference to this point, I should say, that, whether or not the order of Nature is due to a disposing Mind, the hypothesis of mental agency in Nature—or, as the Duke of Argyll terms it, the hypothesis of 'anthropopsychism'—must necessarily have been the earliest hypothesis. What we find in Nature is the universal prevalence of causation, and long before the no less universal equivalency between causes and effects—i.e. the universal prevalence of natural law—became a matter of even the [vaguest] appreciation, the general fact that nothing happens without a cause of some kind was fully recognized. Indeed, the recognition of this fact is not only presented by the lowest races of the present day, but, as I have myself given evidence to show, likewise by animals and infants[21]. And therefore, it appears to me probable that those psychologists are right who argue that the idea of cause is intuitive, in the same sense that the ideas of space and time are intuitive—i.e. the instinctive or [inherited] effect of ancestral experience.

Now if it is thus a matter of certainty that the recognition of causality in Nature is co-extensive with, and even anterior to, the human mind, it appears to me no less certain that the first attempt at assigning a cause of this or that observed event in Nature—i.e. the first attempts at a rational explanation of the phenomena of Nature—must have been of an anthropopsychic kind. No other explanation was, as it were, so ready to hand as that of projecting into external Nature the agency of volition, which was known to each individual as the apparent fountain-head of causal activity so far as he and his neighbours were concerned. To reach this most obvious explanation of causality in Nature, it did not require that primitive man should know, as we know, that the very conception of causality arises out of our sense of effort in voluntary action; it only required that this should be the fact, and then it must needs follow that when any natural phenomenon was thought about at all with reference to its causality, the cause inferred should be one of a psychical kind. I need not wait to trace the gradual integration of this anthropopsychic hypothesis from its earliest and most diffused form of what we may term polypsychism (wherein the causes inferred were almost as personally numerous as the effects contemplated), through polytheism (wherein many effects of a like kind were referred to one deity, who, as it were, took special charge over that class), up to monotheism (wherein all causation is gathered up into the monopsychism of a single personality): it is enough thus briefly to show that from first to last the hypothesis of anthropopsychism is a necessary phase of mental evolution under existing conditions, and this whether or not the hypothesis is true.

Thus viewed, I do not think that 'the general consent of mankind' is a fact of any argumentative weight in favour of the anthropopsychic theory—so far, I mean, as the matter of causation is concerned—whether this be in fetishism or in the teleology of our own day: the general consent of mankind in the larger question of theism (where sundry other matters besides causation fail to be considered) does not here concern us. Indeed, it appears to me that if we are to go back to the savages for any guarantee of our anthropopsychic theory, the pledge which we receive is of worse than no value. As well might we conclude that a match is a living organism, because this is to the mind of a savage the most obvious explanation of its movements, as conclude on precisely similar grounds that our belief in teleology derives any real support from any of the more primitive phases of anthropopsychism.

It seems to me, therefore, that in seeking to estimate the evidence of design in Nature, we must as it were start *de novo*, without reference to anterior beliefs upon the subject. The question is essentially one to be considered in the light of all the latest knowledge that we possess, and by the best faculties of thinking that we (the heirs of all the ages) are able to bring to bear upon it. I shall, therefore, only allude to the history of anthropopsychism in so far as I may find it necessary to do so for the sake of elucidating my argument.

And here it is needful to consider first what Paley called 'the state of the argument' before the Darwinian epoch. This is clearly and tersely presented by Paley in his classical illustration of finding a watch upon a heath—an illustration so well known that I need not here re-state it. I will merely observe, therefore, that it conveys, as it were in one's watch-pocket, the whole of the argument from design; and that it is not in my opinion open to the stricture which was passed upon it by Mill where he says,—'The inference would not be from marks of design, but because I already know by direct experience that watches are made by men.' This appears to me to miss the whole point of Paley's meaning, for there would be obviously no argument at all unless he be understood to mean that the evidence of design which is supposed to be afforded by examination of the watch, is supposed to be afforded by this examination only, and not from any of the direct knowledge alluded to by Mill. For the purposes of the illustration, it must clearly be assumed that the finder of the watch has no previous or direct knowledge touching the manufacture of watches. Apart from this curious misunderstanding, Mill was at one with Paley upon the whole subject.

Again, it is no real objection to the argument or illustration to say, as we often have said, that it does not account for the watchmaker. The object of the argument from design is to *prove* the existence of a designer: not to *explain* that existence. Indeed, it would be suicidal to the whole argument in its relation to Theism, if the possibility of any such explanation were entertained; for such a possibility could only be entertained on the supposition that the being of the Deity admits of being explained—i.e. that the Deity is not ultimate.

Lastly, the argument is precisely the same as that which occurs in numerous passages of Scripture and in theological writings all over the world down to the present time. That is to say, everywhere in organic nature we meet with innumerable adaptations of means to ends, which in very many cases present a degree of refinement and complexity in comparison with which the adaptations of means to ends in a watch are but miserable and rudimentary attempts at mechanism. No one can know so well as the modern biologist in what an immeasurable degree the mechanisms which occur in such profusion in nature surpass, in every form of excellence, the highest triumphs of human invention. Hence at first sight it does unquestionably appear that we could have no stronger or better evidence of purpose than is thus afforded. In the words of Paley: 'arrangement, disposition of parts, subserviency of means to an end, relation of instruments to a use, imply the presence of intelligence and mind.'

But next the question arises, Although such things certainly [may][22] imply the presence of mind as their explanatory cause, are we entitled to assume that there can be in nature no other cause competent to produce these effects? This is a question which never seems to have occurred to Paley, Bell, Chalmers, or indeed to any of the natural theologians up to the time of Darwin. This, I think, is a remarkable fact, because the question is one which, as a mere matter of logical form, appears to lie so much upon the surface. But nevertheless the fact remains that natural theologians, so far as I know without exception, were satisfied to assume as an axiom that mechanism could have no cause other than that of a designing mind; and therefore their work was restricted to tracing out in detail the number and the excellency of the mechanisms which were to be met with in nature. It is, however, obvious that the mere accumulation of such cases can have no real, or logical, effect upon the argument. The mechanisms which we encounter in nature are so amazing in their perfections, that the attentive study of any one of them would (as Paley in his illustration virtually, though not expressly, contends) be sufficient to carry the whole position, if the assumption be conceded that mechanism can only be due to mind. Therefore the argument is not really, or logically, strengthened by the mere accumulation of any number of special cases of mechanism in nature, all as mechanisms similar in kind. Let us now consider this argument.

If we are disposed to wonder why natural theologians prior to the days of Darwin were content to assume that mind is the only possible cause of mechanism, I think we have a ready answer in the universal prevalence of their belief in special creation. For I think it is unquestionable that, upon the basis of this belief, the assumption is legitimate. That is to say, if we start with the belief that all species of plants and animals were originally introduced to the complex conditions of their several environments suddenly and ready made (in some such manner as watches are turned out from a manufactory), then I think we are reasonably entitled to assume that no conceivable cause, other than that of intelligent purpose, could possibly be assigned in explanation of the effects. It is, of course, needless to observe that in so far as this previous belief in special creation was thus allowed to affect the argument from design, that argument became an instance of circular reasoning. And it is, perhaps, equally needless to observe that the mere fact of evolution, as distinguished from special creation—or of the gradual development of living mechanisms, as distinguished from their sudden and ready-made apparition—would not in any way affect the argument from design, unless it could be shown that the process of evolution admits the possibility of some other cause which is not admitted by the hypothesis of special creation. But this is precisely what is shown by the theory of evolution as propounded by Darwin. That is to say, the theory of the gradual development of living mechanisms propounded by Darwin, is something more than a theory of gradual development as distinguished from sudden creation. It is this, but it is also a theory of a purely scientific kind which seeks to explain the purely physical causes of that development. And this is the point where natural science begins to exert her influence upon natural theology—or the point where the theory of evolution begins to affect the theory of design. As this is a most important part of our subject, and one upon which an extraordinary amount of confusion at the present time prevails, I shall in my next paper carefully consider it in all its bearings.

FOOTNOTES:

[19] [The third paper is not published because Romanes' views on the relation between science and faith in Revealed Religion are better and more maturely expressed in the Notes.—ED.]

[20] To avoid misunderstanding I may observe that in the above definitions I am considering Religion and Science under the conditions in which they actually exist. It is conceivable that under other conditions these two departments of thought might not be so sharply separated. Thus, for instance, if a Religion were to appear carrying a revelation to Science upon matters of physical causation, such a Religion (supposing the revelation were found by experiment to be true) ought to be held to exercise upon Science a strictly legitimate influence.

[21] *Mental Evolution in Animals*, pp. 155-8.

[22] [I have put 'may' in place of 'do' for the sake of argument.—ED.]

II.

Suppose the man who found the watch upon a heath to continue his walk till he comes down to the sea-shore, and suppose further that he is as ignorant of physical geography as he is of watch-making. He soon begins to observe a number of adaptations of means to ends, which, if less refined and delicate than those that formed the object of his study in the watch, are on the other hand much more impressive from the greatly larger scale on which they are displayed. First, he observes that there is a beautiful basin hollowed out in the land for the reception of a bay; that the sides of this basin, which from being near its opening are most exposed to the action of large rolling billows, are composed of rocky cliffs, evidently in order to prevent the further encroachment of the sea, and the consequent destruction of the entire bay; that the sides of the basin, which from being successively situated more inland are successively less and less exposed to the action of large waves, are constituted successively of smaller rocks, passing into shingle, and eventually into the finest sand: that as the tides rise and fall with as great a regularity as was exhibited by the movements of the watch, the stones are carefully separated out from the sand to be arranged in sloping layers by themselves, and this always with a most beautiful reference to the places round the margin of the basin which are most in danger of being damaged by the action of the waves. He would further observe, upon closer inspection, that this process of selective arrangement goes into matters of the most minute detail. Here, for instance, he would observe a mile or two of a particular kind of seaweed artistically arranged in one long sinuous line upon the beach; there he would see a wonderful deposit of shells; in another place a lovely little purple heap of garnet sand, the minute particles of which have all been carefully picked out from the surrounding acres of yellow sand. Again, he would notice that the streams which come down to the bay are all flowing in channels admirably dug out for the purpose; and, being led by curiosity to investigate the teleology of these various streams, he would find that they serve to supply the water which the sea loses by evaporation, and also, by a wonderful piece of adjustment, to furnish fresh water to those animals and plants which thrive best in fresh water, and yet by their combined action to carry down sufficient mineral constituents to give that precise degree of saltness to the sea as a whole which is required for the maintenance of pelagic life. Lastly, continuing his investigations along this line of inquiry, he would find that a thousand different habitats were all thoughtfully adapted to the needs of a hundred thousand different forms of life, none of which could survive if these habitats were reversed. Now, I think that our imaginary inquirer would be a dull man if, as the result of all this study, he failed to conclude that the evidence of Design furnished by the marine bay was at least as cogent as that which he had previously found in his study of the watch.

But there is this great difference between the two cases. Whereas by subsequent inquiry he could ascertain as a matter of fact that the watch was due to intelligent contrivance, he could make no such discovery with reference to the marine bay: in the one case intelligent contrivance as a cause is independently demonstrable, while in the other case it can only be inferred. What, then, is the value of the inference?

If, after the studies of our imaginary teleologist had been completed, he were introduced to the library of the Royal Society, and if he were then to spend a year or two in making himself acquainted with the leading results of modern science, I fancy that he would end by being both a wiser and a sadder man. At least I am certain that in learning more he would feel that he is understanding less—that the archaic simplicity of his earlier explanations must give place to a matured perplexity upon the whole subject. To begin with, he would now find that every one of the adjustments of means to ends which excited his admiration on the sea-coast were due to physical causes which are perfectly well understood. The cliffs stood at the opening of the bay because the sea in past ages had encroached upon the coast-line until it met with these cliffs, which then opposed its further progress; the bay was a depression in the land which happened to be there when the sea arrived, and into which the sea consequently flowed; the successive occurrence of rocks, shingle, and sand was due to the actions of the waves themselves; the segregation of sea-weeds, shells, pebbles, and different kinds of sand, was due to their different degrees of specific gravity; the fresh-water streams ran in channels because they had themselves been the means of excavating them; and the multitudinous forms of life were all adapted to their several habitats simply because the unsuited forms were not able to live in them. In all these cases, therefore, our teleologist in the light of fuller knowledge would be compelled to conclude at least this much—that the adaptations which he had so greatly admired when he supposed that they were all due to contrivance in anticipation of the existing phenomena, cease to furnish the same evidence of intelligent design when it is found that no one of them was prepared beforehand by any independent or external cause.

He would therefore be led to conclude that if the teleological interpretation of the facts were to be saved at all, it could only be so by taking a much wider view of the subject than was afforded by the particular cases of apparent design which at first appeared so cogent. That is to say, he would feel that he must abandon the supposition of any *special* design in the construction of that particular bay, and fall back upon the theory of a much more *general* design in the construction of one great scheme of Nature as a whole. In short he would require to dislodge his argument from the special adjustments which in the first instance appeared to him so suggestive, to those general laws of Nature which by their united operation give rise to a cosmos as distinguished from a chaos.

Now I have been careful thus to present in all its more important details an imaginary argument drawn from inorganic nature, because it furnishes a complete analogy to the actual argument which is drawn from organic nature. Without any question, the instances of apparent design, or of the apparently intentional adaptation of means to ends, which we meet with in organic nature, are incomparably more numerous and suggestive than anything with which we meet in inorganic nature. But if once we find good reason to conclude that the former, like the latter, are all due, not to the immediate, special and prospective action of a contriving intelligence (as in watch-making or creation), but to the agency of secondary or physical causes acting under the influence of what we call general laws, then it seems to me that no matter how numerous or how wonderful the adaptations of means to ends in organic nature may be, they furnish one no other or better evidence of design than is furnished by any of the facts of inorganic nature.

For the sake of clearness let us take any special case. Paley says, 'I know of no better method of introducing so large a subject than that of comparing a single thing with a single thing; an eye, for example, with a telescope.' He then goes on to point out the analogies between these two pieces of apparatus, and ends by asking, 'How is it possible, under circumstances of such close affinity, and under the operation of equal evidence, to exclude contrivance in the case of the eye, yet to acknowledge the proof of contrivance having been employed, as the plainest and clearest of all propositions in the case of the telescope?'

Well, the answer to be made is that only upon the hypothesis of special creation can this analogy hold: on the hypothesis of evolution by physical causes the evidence in the two cases is *not* equal. For, upon this hypothesis we have the eye beginning, not as a ready-made structure prepared beforehand for the purposes of seeing, but as a mere differentiation of the ends of nerves in the skin, probably in the first instance to enable them better to discriminate changes of temperature. Pigment having been laid down in these places the better to secure this purpose (I use teleological terms for the sake of brevity), the nerve-ending begins to distinguish between light and darkness. The better to secure this further purpose, the simplest conceivable form of lens begins to appear in the shape of small refractive bodies. Behind these sensory cells are developed, forming the earliest indication of a retina presenting a single layer. And so on, step by step, till we reach the eye of an eagle.

Of course the teleologist will here answer—'The fact of such a gradual building up is no argument against design: whether the structure appeared on a sudden or was the result of a slow elaboration, the marks of design in either case occur in the structure as it stands.' All of which is very true; but I am not maintaining that the fact of a gradual development *in itself* does affect the argument from design. I am maintaining that it only does so because it reveals the possibility (excluded by the hypothesis of sudden or special creation) of the structure having been proximately due to the operation of physical causes. Thus, for the value of argument, let us assume that natural selection has been satisfactorily established as a cause adequate to account for all these effects. Given the facts of heredity, variation, struggle for existence, and the consequent survival of the fittest, what follows? Why that each step in the prolonged and gradual development of the eye was brought about by the elimination of all the less adapted structures in any given generation, i.e. the selection of all the better adapted to perpetuate the improvement by heredity. Will the teleologist maintain that this selective process is itself indicative of special design? If so, it appears to me that he is logically bound to maintain that the long line of seaweed, the shells, the stones and the little heap of garnet sand upon the sea-coast are all equally indicative of special design. The general laws relating to specific gravity are at least of as much importance in the economy of nature as are the general laws relating to specific differentiation; and in each illustration alike we find the result of the operation of known physical causes to be that of selection. If it should be argued in reply that the selection in the one case is obviously purposeless, while in the other it is as obviously purposive, I answer that this is pure assumption. It is perhaps not too much to say that every geological formation on the face of the globe is either wholly or in part due to the selective influence of specific gravity, and who shall say that the construction of the earth's crust is a less important matter in the general scheme of things (if there is such a scheme) than is the evolution of an eye? Or who shall say that because we see an apparently intentional adaptation of means to ends as the result of selection in the case of the eye, there is no intention served by the result of selection in the case of the sea-weeds, stones, sand, mud? For anything that we can know to the contrary, the supposed intelligence may take a greater delight in the latter than in the former process.

For the sake of clearness I have assumed that the physical causes with which we are already acquainted are sufficient to explain the observed phenomena of organic nature. But it clearly makes no difference whether or not this assumption is conceded, provided we allow that the observed phenomena are all due to physical causes of some kind, be they known or unknown. That is to say, in whatever measure we exclude the hypothesis of the direct or immediate intervention of the Deity in organic nature (miracle), in that measure we are reducing the evidence of design in organic nature to precisely the same logical position as that which is occupied by the evidence of design in inorganic nature. Hence I conceive that Mill has shown a singular want of penetration where, after observing with reference to natural selection, 'creative forethought is not absolutely the only link by which the origin of the wonderful mechanism of the eye may be connected with the fact of sight,' he goes on to say, 'leaving this remarkable speculation (i.e. that of natural selection) to whatever fate the progress of discovery may have in store for it, in the present state of knowledge the adaptations in nature afford a large balance of probability in favour of creation by intelligence.' I say this passage seems to me to show a singular want of penetration, and I say so because it appears to argue that the issue lies between the hypothesis of special design and the hypothesis of natural selection. But it does not do so. The issue really lies between special design and natural causes. Survival of the fittest is one of these causes which has been suggested, and shown by a large accumulation of evidence to be probably a true cause. But even if it were to be disproved as a cause, the real argumentative position of teleology would not thereby be effected, unless we were to conclude that there can be no other causes of a secondary or physical kind concerned in the production of the observed adaptations.

I trust that I have now made it sufficiently clear why I hold that if we believe the reign of natural law, or the operation of physical causes, to extend throughout organic nature in the same universal manner as we believe this in the case of inorganic nature, then we can find no better evidence of design in the one province than in the other. The mere fact that we meet with more numerous and apparently more complete instances of design in the one province than in the other is, *ex hypothesi*, merely due to our ignorance of the natural causation in the more intricate province. In studying biological phenomena we are all at present in the intellectual position of our imaginary teleologist when studying the marine bay: we do not know the natural causes which have produced the observed results. But if, after having obtained a partial key in the theory of natural selection, we trust to the large analogy which is afforded by the simpler provinces of Nature, and conclude that physical causes are everywhere concerned in the production of organic structures, then we have concluded that any evidence of design which these structures present is of just the same logical value as that which we may attach to the evidence of design in inorganic nature. If it should still be urged that the adaptations met with in organic nature are from their number and unity much more suggestive of design than anything met with in inorganic nature, I must protest that this is to change the ground of argument and to evade the only point in dispute. No one denies the obvious fact stated: the only question is whether any number and any quantity of adaptations in any one department of nature afford other or better evidence of design than is afforded by adaptations in other departments, when all departments alike are supposed to be equally the outcome of physical causation. And this question I answer in the negative, because we have no means of ascertaining the extent to which the process of natural selection, or any other physical cause, is competent to produce adaptations of the kind observed.

Thus, to take another instance of apparent design from inorganic nature, it has been argued that the constitution of the atmosphere is clearly designed for the support of vegetable and animal life. But before this conclusion can be established upon the facts, it must be shown that life could exist under no other material conditions than those which are furnished to it by the elementary constituents of the atmosphere. This, however, it is clearly impossible to show. For anything that we can know to the contrary, life may actually be existing upon some of the other heavenly bodies under totally different conditions as to atmosphere; and the fact that on this planet all life has come to be dependent upon the gases which occur in our atmosphere, may be due simply to the fact that it was only the forms of life which were able to adapt themselves (through natural selection or other physical causes) to these particular gases which could possibly be expected to occur—just as in matters of still smaller detail, it was only those forms of life that were suited to their several habitats in the marine bay, which could possibly be expected to be found in these several situations. Now, if a set of adjustments so numerous and so delicate as those on which the relations of every known form of life to the constituent gases of the atmosphere are seen to depend, can thus be shown not necessarily to imply the action of any disposing intelligence, how is it possible to conclude that any less general exhibitions of adjustment imply this, so long as every case of adjustment, whether or not ultimately due to design, is regarded as proximately due to physical causes?

In view of these considerations, therefore, I think it is perfectly clear that if the argument from teleology is to be saved at all, it can only be so by shifting it from the narrow basis of special adaptations, to the broad area of Nature as a whole. And here I confess that to my mind the argument does acquire a weight which, if long and attentively considered, deserves to be regarded as enormous. For, although this and that particular adjustment in Nature may be seen to be proximately due to physical causes, and although we are prepared on the grounds of the largest possible analogy to infer that all other such particular cases are likewise due to physical causes, the more ultimate question arises, How is it that all physical causes conspire, by their united action, to the production of a general order of Nature? It is against all analogy to suppose that such an end as this can be accomplished by such means as those, in the way of mere chance or 'the fortuitous concourse of atoms.' We are led by the most fundamental dictates of our reason to conclude that there must be some cause for this co-operation of causes. I know that from Lucretius' time this has been denied; but it has been denied only on grounds of *feeling*. No possible *reason* can be given for the denial which does not run counter to the law of causation itself. I am therefore perfectly clear that the only question which, from a purely rational point of view, here stands to be answered is this—Of what nature are we to suppose the *causa causarum* to be?

On this point only two hypotheses have ever been advanced, and I think it is impossible to conceive that any third one is open. Of these two hypotheses the earliest, and of course the most obvious, is that of mental purpose. The other hypothesis is one which we owe to the far-reaching thought of Mr. Herbert Spencer. In Chapter VII of his *First Principles* he argues that all causation arises immediately out of existence as such, or, as he states it, that 'uniformity of law inevitably follows from the persistence of force.' For 'if in any two cases there is exact likeness not only between those most conspicuous antecedents which we distinguish as the causes, but also between those accompanying antecedents which we call the conditions, we cannot affirm that the effects will differ, without affirming either that some force has come into existence or that some force has ceased to exist. If the co-operative forces in the one case are equal to those in the other, each to each, in distribution and amount; then it is impossible to conceive the product of their joint action in the one case as unlike that in the other, without conceiving one or more of the forces to have increased or diminished in quantity; and this is conceiving that force is not persistent.'

Now this interpretation of causality as the immediate outcome of existence must be considered first as a theory of causation, and next as a theory in relation to Theism. As a theory of causation it has not met with the approval of mathematicians, physicists, or logicians, leading representatives of all these departments of thought having expressly opposed it, while, so far as I am aware, no representative of any one of them has spoken in its favour[23]. But with this point I am not at present concerned, for even if the theory were admitted to furnish a full and complete explanation of causality, it would still fail to account for the harmonious relation of causes, or the fact with which we are now alone concerned. This distinction is not perceived by the anonymous author 'Physicus,' who, in his *Candid Examination of Theism*, lays great stress upon Mr. Spencer's theory of causation as subversive of Theism, or at least as superseding the necessity of theistic hypothesis by furnishing a full explanation of the order of Nature on purely physical grounds. But he fails to perceive that even if Mr. Spencer's theory were conceded fully to explain all the facts of causality, it would in no wise tend to explain the cosmos in which these facts occur. It may be true that causation depends upon the 'persistence of force': it does not follow that all manifestations of force should on this account have been directed to occur as they do occur. For, if we follow back any sequence of physical causation, we soon find that it spreads out on all sides into a network of physical relations which are literally infinite both in space (conditions) and in time (antecedent causes). Now, even if we suppose that the persistence of force is a sufficient explanation of the occurrence of the particular sequence contemplated so far as the exhibition of force is there concerned, we are thus as far as ever from explaining the *determination* of this force into the particular channel through which it flows. It may be quite true that the resultant is determined as to magnitude and direction by the components; but what about the magnitude and direction of the components? If it is said that they in turn were determined by the outcome of previous systems, how about these systems? And so on till we spread away into the infinite network already mentioned. Only if we knew the origin of all series of all such systems could we be in a position to say that an adequate intelligence might determine beforehand by calculation the state of any one part of the universe at any given instant of time. But, as the series are infinite both in number and extent, this knowledge is clearly out of the question. Moreover, even if it could be imagined as possible, it could only be so imagined at the expense of supposing an origin of physical causation in time; and this amounts to supposing a state of things prior to such causation, and out of which it arose. But to suppose this is to suppose some extra-physical source of physical causation; and whether this supposition is made with reference to a physical event occurring under immediate observation (miracle), or to a physical event in past time, or to the origin of all physical events, it is alike incompatible with any theory that seeks to give a purely physical explanation of the physical universe as a whole. It is, in short, the old story about a stream not being able to rise above its source. Physical causation cannot be made to supply its own explanation, and the mere persistence of force, even if it were conceded to account for particular cases of physical sequence, can give no account of the ubiquitous and eternal direction of force in the construction and maintenance of universal order.

We are thus, as it were, driven upon the theory of Theism as furnishing the only nameable explanation of this universal order. That is to say, by no logical artifice can we escape from the conclusion that, as far as we can see, this universal order must be regarded as due to some one integrating principle; and that this, so far as we can see, is most probably of the nature of mind. At least it must be allowed that we can conceive of it under no other aspect; and that if any particular adaptation in organic nature is held to be suggestive of such an agency, the sum total of all adaptations in the universe must be held to be incomparably more so. I shall not, however, dwell upon this theme since it has been well treated by several modern writers, and with special cogency by the Rev. Baden Powell. I will merely observe that I do not consider it necessary to the display of this argument in favour of Theism that we should speak of 'natural laws.' It is enough to take our stand upon the [broadest] general fact that Nature is a system, and that the order observable in this system is absolutely universal, eternally enduring, and infinitely exact; while only upon the supposition of its being such is our experience conceived as possible, or our knowledge conceived as attainable.

Having thus stated as emphatically as I can that in my opinion no explanation of natural order can be either conceived or named other than that of intelligence as the supreme directing cause, I shall proceed to two other questions which arise immediately out of this conclusion. The first of these questions is as to the presumable character of this supreme Intelligence so far as any data of inference upon this point are supplied by our observation of Nature; and the other question is as to the strictly formal cogency of any conclusions either with reference to the existence or the character of such an intelligence[24]. I shall consider these two points separately.

No sooner have we reached the conclusion that the only hypothesis whereby the general order of Nature admits of being in any degree accounted for is that it is due to a cause of a mental kind, than we confront the fact that this cause must be widely different from anything that we know of Mind in ourselves. And we soon discover that this difference must be conceived as not merely of degree, however great, but of kind. In other words, although we may conclude that the nearest analogue of the *causa causarum* given in experience is the human mind, we are bound to acknowledge that in all fundamental points the analogy is so remote that it becomes a question whether we are really very much nearer the truth by entertaining it. Thus, for instance, as Mr. Spencer has pointed out, our only conception of that which we know as Mind in ourselves is the conception of a series of states of consciousness. But, he continues, 'Put a series of states of consciousness as cause and the evolving universe as effect, and then endeavour to see the last as flowing from the first. I find it possible to imagine in some dim way a series of states of consciousness serving as antecedent to any one of the movements I see going on; for my own states of consciousness are often indirectly the antecedents to such movements. But how if I attempt to think of such a series as antecedent to *all* actions throughout the universe ...? If to account for this infinitude of physical changes everywhere going on, "Mind must be conceived as there," "under the guise of simple-dynamics," then the reply is, that, to be so conceived, Mind must be divested of all attributes by which it is distinguished; and that, when thus divested of its distinguishing attributes the conception disappears—the word Mind stands for a blank.'

Moreover, 'How is the "originating Mind" to be thought of as having states produced by things objective to it, as discriminating among these states, and classing them as like and unlike; and as preferring one objective result to another?'[25]

Hence, without continuing this line of argument, which it would not be difficult to trace through every constituent branch of human psychology, we may take it as unquestionable that, if there is a Divine Mind, it must differ so essentially from the human mind, that it becomes illogical to designate the two by the same name: the attributes of eternity and ubiquity are in themselves enough to place such a Mind in a category *sui generis*, wholly different from anything which the analogy furnished by our own mind enables us even dimly to conceive. And this, of course, is no more than theologians admit. God's thoughts are above our thoughts, and a God who would be comprehensible to our intelligence would be no God at all, they say. Which may be true enough, only we must remember that in whatever measure we are thus precluded from understanding the Divine Mind, in that measure are we precluded from founding any conclusions as to its nature upon analogies furnished by the human mind. The theory ceases to be anthropomorphic: it ceases to be even 'anthropopsychic': it is affiliated with the conception of mind only in virtue of the one fact that it serves to give the best provisional account of the order of Nature, by supposing an infinite extension of some of the faculties of the human mind, with a concurrent obliteration of all the essential conditions under which alone these faculties are known to exist. Obviously of such a Mind as this no predication is logically possible. If such a Mind exists, it is not conceivable as existing, and we are precluded from assigning to it any attributes.

Thus much on general grounds. Descending now to matters of more detail, let us assume with the natural theologians that such a Mind does exist, that it so far resembles the human mind as to be a conscious, personal intelligence, and that the care of such a Mind is over all its works. Even upon the grounds of this supposition we meet with a number of large and general facts which indicate that this Mind ought still to be regarded as apparently very unlike its 'image' in the mind of man. I will not here dwell upon the argument of seeming waste and purposeless action in Nature, because I think that this may be fairly met by the ulterior argument already drawn from Nature as a whole—viz. that as a whole, Nature is a cosmos, and therefore that what to us appears wasteful and purposeless in matters of detail may not be so in relation to the scheme of things as a whole. But I am doubtful whether this ulterior argument can fairly be adduced to meet the apparent absence in Nature of that which in man we term morality. For in the human mind the sense of right and wrong—with all its accompanying or constituting emotions of love, sympathy, justice, &c.—is so important a factor, that however greatly we may imagine the intellectual side of the human mind to be extended, we can scarcely imagine that the moral side could ever become so apparently eclipsed as to end in the authorship of such a work as we find in terrestrial nature. It is useless to hide our eyes to the state of matters which meets us here. Most of the instances of special design which are relied upon by the natural theologian to prove the intelligent nature of the First Cause, have as their end or object the infliction of painful death or the escape from remorseless enemies; and so far the argument in favour of the intelligent nature of the First Cause is an argument against its morality. Again, even if we quit the narrower basis on which teleological argument has rested in the past, and stand that argument upon the broader ground of Nature as a whole, it scarcely becomes less incompatible with any inference to the morality of that Cause, seeing that the facts to which I have alluded are not merely occasional and, as it were, outweighed by contrary facts of a more general kind, but manifestly constitute the leading feature of the scheme of organic nature as a whole: or, if this were held to be questionable, it could only follow that we are not entitled to infer that there is any such scheme at all.

Nature, as red in tooth and claw with ravin, is thus without question a large and general fact that must be considered by any theory of teleology which can be propounded. I do not think that this aspect of the matter could be conveyed in stronger terms than it is by 'Physicus[26],' whom I shall therefore quote:—

'Supposing the Deity to be, what Professor Flint maintains that he is—viz. omnipotent, and there can be no inference more transparent than that such wholesale suffering, for whatever ends designed, exhibits an incalculably greater deficiency of beneficence in the divine character than that which we know in any, the very worst, of human characters. For let us pause for one moment to think of what suffering in Nature means. Some hundreds of millions of years ago some millions of millions of animals must be supposed to have become sentient. Since that time till the present, there must have been millions and millions of generations of millions and millions of individuals. And throughout all this period of incalculable duration, this inconceivable host of sentient organisms have been in a state of unceasing battle, dread, ravin, pain. Looking to the outcome, we find that more than one half of the species which have survived the ceaseless struggle are parasitic in their habits, lower and insentient forms of life feasting on higher and sentient forms; we find teeth and talons whetted for slaughter, hooks and suckers moulded for torment—everywhere a reign of terror, hunger, sickness, with oozing blood and quivering limbs, with gasping breath and eyes of innocence that dimly close in deaths of cruel torture! Is it said that there are compensating enjoyments? I care not to strike the balance; the enjoyments I plainly perceive to be as physically necessary as the pains, and this whether or not evolution is due to design.... Am I told that I am not competent to judge the purposes of the Almighty? I answer that if there are *purposes*, I *am* able to judge of them so far as I can see; and if I am expected to judge of His purposes when they appear to be beneficent, I am in consistency obliged also to judge of them when they appear to be malevolent.

And it can be no possible extenuation of the latter to point to the "final result" as "order and beauty," so long as the means adopted by the "*Omnipotent Designer*" are known to have been so [terrible]. All that we could legitimately assert in this case would be that, so far as observation can extend, "He cares for animal perfection" *to the exclusion of* "animal enjoyment," and even to the *total disregard* of animal suffering. But to assert this would merely be to deny beneficence as an attribute of God[27].'

The reasoning here appears as unassailable as it is obvious. If, as the writer goes on to say, we see a rabbit panting in the iron jaws of a spring trap, and in consequence abhor the devilish nature of the being who, with full powers of realizing what pain means, can deliberately employ his whole faculties of invention in contriving a thing so hideously cruel; what are we to think of a Being who, with yet higher faculties of thought and knowledge, and with an unlimited choice of means to secure His ends, has contrived untold thousands of mechanisms no less diabolical? In short, so far as Nature can teach us, or 'observation can extend,' it does appear that the scheme, if it is a scheme, is the product of a Mind which differs from the more highly evolved type of human mind in that it is immensely more intellectual without being nearly so moral. And the same thing is indicated by the rough and indiscriminate manner in which justice is allotted—even if it can be said to be allotted at all. When we contrast the certainty and rigour with which any offence against 'physical law' is punished by Nature (no matter though the sin be but one of ignorance), with the extreme uncertainty and laxity with which she meets any offence against 'moral law,' we are constrained to feel that the system of legislation (if we may so term it) is conspicuously different from that which would have been devised by any intelligence which in any sense could be called 'anthropopsychic.'

The only answer to these difficulties open to the natural theologian is that which is drawn from the constitution of the human mind. It is argued that the fact of this mind having so large an ingredient of morality in its constitution may be taken as proof that its originating source is likewise of a moral character. This argument, however, appears to me of a questionable character, seeing that, for anything we can tell to the contrary, the moral sense may have been given to, or developed in, man simply on account of its utility to the species—just in the same way as teeth in the shark or poison in the snake. If so, the occurrence of the moral sense in man would merely furnish one other instance of the intellectual, as distinguished from the moral, nature of God; and there seems to be in itself no reason why we should take any other view. The mere fact that to *us* the moral sense seems such a great and holy thing, is doubtless (under any view) owing to its importance to the well-being of our species. In itself, or as it appears to other possible beings intellectual like ourselves, but existing under unlike conditions, the moral sense of man may be regarded as of no more significance than the social instincts of bees. More particularly may this consideration apply to the case of a Mind existing, according to the theological theory of things, wholly beyond the pale of anything analogous to those social relations out of which, according to the scientific theory of evolution, the moral sense has been developed in ourselves[28].

The truth is that in this matter natural theologians begin by assuming that the First Cause, if intelligent, *must* be moral; and then they are blinded to the strictly logical weakness of the argument whereby they endeavour to sustain their assumption. For aught that we can tell to the contrary, it may be quite as 'anthropomorphic' a notion to attribute morality to God as it would be to attribute those capacities for sensuous enjoyment with which the Greeks endowed their divinities. The Deity may be as high above the one as the other—or rather perhaps we may say as much external to the one as to the other. Without being supra-moral, and still less immoral, He may be un-moral: our ideas of morality may have no meaning as applied to Him.

But if we go thus far in one direction, I think, *per contra*, it must in consistency be allowed that the argument from the constitution of the human mind acquires more weight when it is shifted from the moral sense to the religious instincts. For, on the one hand, these instincts are not of such obvious use to the species as are those of morality; and, on the other hand, while they are unquestionably very general, very persistent, and very powerful, they do not appear to serve any 'end' or 'purpose' in the scheme of things, unless we accept the theory which is given of them by those in whom they are most strongly developed. Here I think we have an argument of legitimate force, although it does not appear that such was the opinion entertained of it by Mill. I think the argument is of legitimate force, because if the religious instincts of the human race point to no reality as their object, they are out of analogy with all other instinctive endowments. Elsewhere in the animal kingdom we never meet with such a thing as an instinct pointing aimlessly, and therefore the fact of man being, as it is said, 'a religious animal'—i.e. presenting a class of feelings of a peculiar nature directed to particular ends, and most akin to, if not identical with, true instinct—is so far, in my opinion, a legitimate argument in favour of the reality of some object towards which the religious side of this animal's nature is directed. And I do not think that this argument is invalidated by such facts as that widely different intellectual conceptions touching the character of this object are entertained by different races of mankind; that the force of the religious instincts differs greatly in different individuals even of the same race; that these instincts admit of being greatly modified by education; that they would probably fail to be developed in any individual without at least so much education as is required to furnish the needful intellectual conceptions on which they are founded; or that we may not improbably trace their origin, as Mr. Spencer traces it, to a primitive mode of interpreting dreams. For even in view of all these considerations the fact remains that these instincts *exist*, and therefore, like all other instincts, may be supposed to have a *definite* meaning, even though, like all other instincts, they may be supposed to have had a *natural cause*, which both in the individual and in the race requires, as in the natural development of all other instincts, the natural conditions for its occurrence to be supplied. In a word, if animal instincts generally, like organic structures or inorganic systems, are held to betoken purpose, the religious nature of man would stand out as an anomaly in the general scheme of things if it alone were purposeless. Hence we have here what seems to me a valid inference, so far as it goes, to the effect that, if the general order of Nature is due to Mind, the character of that Mind is such as it is conceived to be by the most highly developed form of religion. A conclusion which is no doubt the opposite of that which we reached by contemplating the phenomena of biology; and a contradiction which can only be overcome by supposing, either that Nature conceals God, while man reveals Him, or that Nature reveals God while man misrepresents Him.

There is still one other fact of a very wide and general kind presented by Nature, which, if the order of Nature is taken to be the expression of intelligent purpose, ought in my opinion to be regarded as of great weight in furnishing evidence upon the ethical quality of that purpose. It is a fact which, so far as I know, has not been considered by any other writer; but from its being one of the most general of all the facts relating to the sentient creation, and from its admitting of no one single exception, I feel that I am not able too strongly to emphasize its argumentative importance. This fact is, as I have stated it on a former occasion, 'that amid all the millions of mechanisms and instincts in the animal kingdom, there is no one instance of a mechanism or instinct occurring in one species for the exclusive benefit of another species, although there are a few cases in which a mechanism or instinct that is of benefit to its possessor has come also to be utilized by other species. Now, on the beneficent design theory it is impossible to explain why, when all the mechanisms in the same species are invariably correlated for the benefit of that species, there should never be any such correlation between mechanisms in different species, or why the same remark should apply to instincts. For how magnificent a display of Divine beneficence would organic nature have afforded, if all, or even some, species had been so inter-related as to minister to each other's necessities. Organic species might then have been likened to a countless multitude of voices all singing in one harmonious psalm of praise. But, as it is, we see no vestige of such co-ordination; every species is for itself, and for itself alone—an outcome of the always and everywhere fiercely raging struggle for life[29].'

The large and general fact thus stated constitutes, in my opinion, the strongest of all arguments in favour of Mr. Darwin's theory of natural selection, and therefore we can see the probable reason why it is what it is, so far as the question of its physical causation is concerned. But where the question is, Supposing the physical causation ultimately due to Mind, what are we to infer concerning the character of the Mind which has adopted this method of causation?—then we again reach the answer that, so far as we can judge from a conscientious examination of these facts, this Mind does not show that it is of a nature which in man we should call moral. Of course behind the physical appearances there may be a moral justification, so that from these appearances we are not entitled to say more than that from the fact of its having chosen a method of physical causation leading to these results, it has presented to us the appearance, as before observed, of caring for animal perfection to the exclusion of animal enjoyment, and even to the total disregard of animal suffering.

In conclusion, it is of importance to insist upon a truth which in discussions of this kind is too often disregarded—viz. that all our reasonings being of a character relative to our knowledge, our inferences are uncertain in a degree proportionate to the extent of our ignorance; and that as with reference to the topics which we have been considering our ignorance is of immeasurable extent, any conclusions that we may have formed are, as Bishop Butler would say, 'infinitely precarious.' Or, as I have previously presented this formal aspect of the matter while discussing the teleological argument with Professor Asa Gray,—'I suppose it will be admitted that the validity of an inference depends upon the number, the importance, and the definiteness of the things or ratios known, as compared with the number, importance, and definiteness of the things or ratios unknown, but inferred. If so, we should be logically cautious in drawing inferences from the natural to the supernatural: for although we have the entire sphere of experience from which to draw an inference, we are unable to gauge the probability of the inference when drawn—the unknown ratios being confessedly of unknown number, importance, and degree of definiteness: the whole orbit of human knowledge is insufficient to obtain a parallax whereby to institute the required measurements or to determine the proportion between the terms known and the terms unknown. Otherwise phrased, we may say—as our knowledge of a part is to our knowledge of a whole, so is our inference from that part to the reality of that whole. Who, therefore, can say, even upon the hypothesis of Theism, that our inferences or "idea of design" would have any meaning if applied to the "All-Upholder," whose thoughts are not as our thoughts?'[30] And of course, *mutatis mutandis*, the same remarks apply to all inferences having a negative tendency.

As an outcome of the whole of this discussion, then, I think it appears that the influence of Science upon Natural Religion has been uniformly of a destructive character. Step by step it has driven back the apparent evidence of direct or special design in Nature, until now this evidence resides exclusively in the one great and general fact that Nature as a whole is a Cosmos. Further than this it is obviously impossible that the destructive influence of Science can extend, because Science can only exist upon the basis of this fact. But when we allow that this great and universal fact—which but for the effects of unremitting familiarity could scarcely fail to be intellectually overwhelming—does betoken mental agency in Nature, we immediately find it impossible to determine the probable character of such a mind, even supposing that it exists. We cannot conceive of it as presenting any one of the qualities which essentially characterize what we know as mind in ourselves; and therefore the word Mind, as applied to the supposed agency, stands for a blank. Further, even if we disregard this difficulty, and assume that in some way or other incomprehensible to us a Mind does exist as far transcending the human mind as the human mind transcends mechanical motion; still we are met by some very large and general facts in Nature which seem strongly to indicate that this Mind, if it exists, is either deficient in, or wholly destitute of, that class of feelings which in man we term moral; while, on the other hand, the religious aspirations of man himself may be taken to indicate the opposite conclusion. And, lastly, with reference to the whole course of such reasonings, we have seen that any degree of measurable probability, as attaching to the conclusions, is unattainable. From all which it appears that Natural Religion at the present time can only be regarded as a system full of intellectual contradictions and moral perplexities; so that if we go to her with these greatest of all questions: 'Is there knowledge with the Most High?' 'Shall not the Judge of all the earth do right?' the only clear answer which we receive is the one that comes back to us from the depths of our own heart—'When I thought upon this it was too painful for me.'

FOOTNOTES:

[23] A note (of 1893) contains the following: 'Being, considered in the abstract, is logically equivalent to Not-Being or Nothing. For if by successive stages of abstraction, we divest the conception of Being of attribute and relation we reach the conception of that which cannot be, i.e. a logical contradiction, or the logical correlative of Being which is Nothing. (All this is well expressed in Caird's *Evolution of Religion.*) The failure to perceive this fact constitutes a ground fallacy in my *Candid Examination of Theism*, where I represent Being as being a sufficient explanation of the Order of Nature or the law of Causation.'

[24] This promise is only partially fulfilled in the penultimate paragraph of the essay.—ED.

[25] *Essays*, vol. iii. p. 246 et seq. The whole passage ought to be consulted, being too long to quote here.

[26] In an essay on Prof. Flint's *Theism*, appended to the *Candid Examination.*

[27] *A Candid Examination of Theism*, pp. 171-2.

[28] [I have, as Editor, resisted a temptation to intervene in the above argument. But I think I may intervene on a matter of fact, and point out that 'according to the theological theory of things,' i.e. according to the Trinitarian doctrine, God's Nature consists in what is strictly 'analogous to social relations,' and He not merely exhibits in His creation, but Himself *is* Love. See, on the subject, especially, R.H. Hutton's essay on the Incarnation, in his *Theological Essays* (Macmillan).—ED.]

[29] *Scientific Evidences of Organic Evolution*, pp. 76-7.

[30] *Nature*, April 5, 1883.

PART II.

Introductory Note by the Editor.

Little more requires to be said by way of introduction to the Notes which are all that George Romanes was able to write of a work that was to have been entitled *A Candid Examination of Religion.* What little does require to be said must be by way of bridging the interval of thought which exists between the Essays which have just preceded and the Notes which represent more nearly his final phase of mind.

The most anti-theistic feature in the Essays is the stress laid in them on the evidence which Nature supplies, or is supposed to supply, antagonistic to the belief in the goodness of God.

On this mysterious and perplexing subject George Romanes appears to have had more to say but did not live to say it[31]. We may notice however that in 1889, in a paper read before the Aristotelian Society, on 'the Evidence of Design in Nature[32],' he appears to allow more weight than before to the argument that the method of physical development must be judged in the light of its result. This paper was part of a *Symposium.* Mr. S. Alexander has argued in a previous paper against the hypothesis of 'design' in Nature on the ground that 'the fair order of Nature is only acquired by a wholesale waste and sacrifice.' This argument was developed by pointing to the obvious 'mal-adjustments,' 'aimless destructions,' &c., which characterize the processes of Nature. But these, Romanes replies, necessarily belong to the process considered as one of 'natural selection.' The question is only: Is such a process *per se* incompatible with the hypothesis of design? And he replies in the negative.

'"The fair order of Nature is only acquired by a wholesale waste and sacrifice." Granted. But if the "wholesale waste and sacrifice," as antecedent, leads to a "fair order of Nature" as its consequent, how can it be said that the "wholesale waste and sacrifice" has been a failure? Or how can it be said that, in point of fact, there *has* been a waste, or *has* been a sacrifice? Clearly such things can only be said when our point of view is restricted to the means (i.e. the wholesale destruction of the less fit); not when we extend our view to what, even within the limits of human observation, is unquestionably the *end* (i.e. the causal result in an ever improving world of types). A candidate who is plucked in a Civil Service examination because he happens to be one of the less fitted to pass, is no doubt an instance of failure so far as his own career is concerned; but it does not therefore follow that the system of examination is a failure in its final end of securing the best men for the Civil Service. And the fact that the general outcome of all the individual failures in Nature is that of securing what Mr. Alexander calls "the fair order of Nature," is assuredly evidence that the *modus operandi* has not been a failure in relation to what, if there be any Design in Nature at all, must be regarded as the higher purpose of such Design. Therefore, cases of individual or otherwise relative failure cannot be quoted as evidence against the hypothesis of there being such Design. The fact that the general system of natural causation has for its eventual result "a fair order of Nature," cannot of itself be a fact inimical to the hypothesis of Design in Nature, even though it be true that such causation entails the continual elimination of the less efficient types.

'To the best of my judgement, then, this argument from failure, random trial, blind blundering, or in whatever other terminology the argument may be presented, is only valid as against the theory of what Mr. Alexander alludes to as a "Carpenter-God," i.e. that if there be Design in Nature at all, it must everywhere be *special* Design; so that the evidence of it may as well be tested by any given minute fragment of Nature—such as one individual organism or class of organisms—as by having regard to the whole Cosmos. The evidence of Design in this sense I fully allow has been totally destroyed by the proof of natural selection. But such destruction has only brought into clearer relief the much larger question that rises behind, viz. as before phrased, Is there anything about the method of natural causation, considered as a whole, that is inimical to the theory of Design in Nature, considered as a whole?'

It is true that this argument does not bear directly upon the *character* of the God whose 'design' Nature exhibits: but indirectly it does[33]. For instance, such an argument as that found above (on p. 79: 'we see a rabbit, &c.') seems to be only valid on the postulate here described as that of the 'Carpenter-God.'

It is also probable that Romanes felt the difficulty arising from the cruelty of nature less, as he was led to dwell more on humanity as the most important part of nature, and perceived the function of suffering in the economy of human life (pp. 142, 154): and also as he became more impressed with the positive evidences for Christianity as at once the religion of sorrow and the revelation of God as Love (pp. 163, ff.). The Christian Faith supplies believers not only with an argument against pessimism from general results, but also with such an insight into the Divine character and method as enables them at least to bear hopefully the awful perplexities which arise from the spectacle of individuals suffering.

In the last year or two of his life he read very attentively a great number of books on 'Christian Evidences,' from Pascal's *Pensées* downwards, and studied carefully the appearance of 'plan' in the Biblical Revelation considered as a whole. The *fact* of this study appears in fragmentary remarks, indices and references, which George Romanes left behind him in note-books. The *results* of it will not be unapparent in the following Notes, which, I need to remind my readers, are, in spite of their small bulk, the sole reason for the existence of this volume.

In reading these I can hardly conceive any one not being possessed with a profound regret that the author was not allowed to complete his work. And it is only fair to ask every reader of the following pages to remember that he is reading, in the main, incomplete notes and not finished work. This will account for a great deal that may seem sketchy and unsatisfactory in the treatment of different points, and also for repetitions and traces of inconsistency. But I can hardly think any one can read these notes to the end without agreeing with me that if I had withheld them from publication, the world would have lost the witness of a mind, both able and profoundly sincere, feeling after God and finding Him.

C.G.

FOOTNOTES:

[31] See below, and note. I find also the following note of a date subsequent to 1889. 'It is a fact that pessimism is illogical, simply because we are inadequate judges of the world, and pessimism would therefore be opposed to agnosticism. We may know that there is something out of joint between the world and ourselves; but we cannot know how far this is the fault of the world or of ourselves.'

[32] *Proceedings of the Aristotelian Society* (Williams & Norgate), vol. i. no. 3, pp. 72, 73.

[33] I ought also to mention that Romanes on the Sunday before his death expressed to me verbally his entire agreement with the argument of Professor Knight's *Aspects of Theism* (Macmillan, 1893); in which on this subject see pp. 184-186, 'A larger good is evolved through the winnowing process by which physical nature casts its weaker products aside,' &c.

NOTES FOR A WORK ON A CANDID EXAMINATION OF RELIGION.

BY METAPHYSICUS.

Proposed Mottoes.

'I quite admit the difficulty of believing that in every man there is an eye of the soul which, when by other pursuits lost and dimmed, is by this purified and re-illumined; and is more precious far than ten thousand bodily eyes, for by this alone is truth seen. Now there are two classes of persons, one class who will agree with you and will take your words as a revelation; another class who have no understanding of them and to whom they will naturally be as idle tales.

'And you had better decide at once with which of the two you are arguing; or, perhaps, you will say with neither, and that your chief aim in carrying on the argument is your own improvement; at the same time not grudging to either any benefit which they may derive.'—PLATO.

'If we would reprove with success, and show another his mistake, we must see from what side he views the matter, for on that side it is generally true: and, admitting this truth, show him the side on which it is false.'—PASCAL.

---

§ 1. INTRODUCTORY.

Many years ago I published in Messrs. Trübner's 'Philosophical Series,' a short treatise entitled *A Candid Examination of Theism* by 'Physicus.' Although the book made some stir at the time, and has since exhibited a vitality never anticipated by its author, the secret of its authorship has been well preserved[34]. This secret it is my intention, if possible, still to preserve; but as it is desirable (on several accounts which will become apparent in the following pages) to avow identity of authorship, the present essay appears under the same pseudonym[35] as its predecessor. The reason why the first essay appeared anonymously is truthfully stated in the preface thereof, viz. in order that the reasoning should be judged on its own merits, without the bias which is apt to arise on the part of a reader from a knowledge of the authority—or absence of authority—on the part of a writer. This reason, in my opinion, still holds good as regards *A Candid Examination of Theism*, and applies in equal measure to the present sequel in *A Candid Examination of Religion.*

It will be shown that in many respects the negative conclusions reached in the former essay have been greatly modified by the results of maturer thought as now presented in the second. Therefore it seems desirable to state at the outset that, as far as I am capable of judging, the modifications in question have not been due in any measure to influence from without. They appear to have been due exclusively to the results of my own further thought, as briefly set out in the following pages, with no indebtedness to private friends and but little to published utterances in the form of books, &c. Nevertheless, no very original ideas are here presented. Indeed, I suppose it would nowadays be impossible to present any idea touching religion, which has not at some time or another been presented previously. Still much may be done in the furthering of one's thought by changing points of view, selecting and arranging ideas already more or less familiar, so that they may be built into new combinations; and this, I think, I have in no small degree accomplished as regards the microcosm of my own mind. But I state this much only for the sake of adding a confession that, as far as introspection can carry one, it does not appear to me that the modifications which my views have undergone since the publication of my previous *Candid Examination* are due so much to purely logical processes of the intellect, as to the sub-conscious (and therefore more or less unanalyzable) influences due to the ripening experience of life. The extent to which this is true [i.e. the extent to which experience modifies logic][36] is seldom, if ever, realized, although it is practically exemplified every day by the sobering caution which advancing age exercises upon the mind. Not so much by any above-board play of syllogism as by some underhand cheating of consciousness, do the accumulating experiences of life and of thought slowly enrich the judgement. And this, one need hardly say, is especially true in such regions of thought as present the most tenuous media for the progress of thought by the comparatively clumsy means of syllogistic locomotion. For the further we ascend from the solid ground of verification, the less confidence should we place in our wings of speculation, while the more do we find the practical wisdom of such intellectual caution, or distrust of ratiocination, as can be given only by experience. Therefore, most of all is this the case in those departments of thought which are furthest from the region of our sensuous life—viz. metaphysics and religion. And, as a matter of fact, it is just in these departments of thought that we find the rashness of youth most amenable to the discipline in question by the experience of age.

However, in spite of this confession, I have no doubt that even in the matter of pure and conscious reason further thought has enabled me to detect serious errors, or rather oversights, in the very foundations of my *Candid Examination of Theism.* I still think, indeed, that from the premises there laid down the conclusions result in due logical sequence, so that, as a matter of mere ratiocination, I am not likely ever to detect any serious flaws, especially as this has not been done by anybody else during the many years of its existence. But I now clearly perceive two wellnigh fatal oversights which I then committed. The first was undue confidence in merely syllogistic conclusions, even when derived from sound premises, in regions of such high abstraction. The second was, in not being sufficiently careful in examining the foundations of my criticism, i.e. the validity of its premises. I will here briefly consider these two points separately.

As regards the first point, never was any one more arrogant in his claims for pure reason than I was—more arrogant in spirit though not in letter, this being due to contact with science; without ever considering how opposed to reason itself is the unexpressed assumption of my earlier argument as to God Himself, as if His existence were a merely physical problem to be solved by man's reason alone, without reference to his other and higher faculties[37].

The second point is of still more importance, because so seldom, if ever, recognized.

At the time of writing the *Candid Examination* I perceived clearly how the whole question of Theism from the side of reason turned on the question as to the nature of natural causation. My theory of natural causation obeyed the Law of Parsimony, resolving all into Being as such; but, on the other hand, it erred in not considering whether 'higher causes' are not 'necessary' to account for spiritual facts—i.e. whether the ultimate Being must not be at least as high as the intellectual and spiritual nature of man, i.e. higher than anything merely physical or mechanical. The supposition that it must does not violate the Law of Parsimony.

Pure agnostics ought to investigate the religious consciousness of Christians as a phenomenon which may possibly be what Christians themselves believe it to be, i.e. of Divine origin. And this may be done without entering into any question as to the objective validity of Christian dogmas. The metaphysics of Christianity may be all false in fact, and yet the spirit of Christianity may be true in substance—i.e. it may be the highest 'good gift from above' as yet given to man.

My present object, then, like that of Socrates, is not to impart any philosophical system, or even positive knowledge, but a frame of mind, what I may term, pure agnosticism, as distinguished from what is commonly so called.

FOOTNOTES:

[34] The first edition, which was published in 1878, was rapidly exhausted, but, as my object in publishing was solely that of soliciting criticism for my own benefit, I arranged with the publishers not to issue any further edition. The work has therefore been out of print for many years.

[This 'arrangement' was however not actually made, or at least was unknown to the present publishing firm of Kegan Paul, Trench, Trübner & Co. Thus a new edition of the book was published in 1892, to the author's surprise.—ED.]

[35] [Or rather it was intended that it should appear under the pseudonym of 'Metaphysicus.'—ED.]

[36] [Words in square brackets have been added by me. But I have not introduced the brackets when I have simply inserted single unimportant words obviously necessary for the sense.—ED.]

[37] [See p. 29, quotation from Preface of 'Physicus.' The state of mind expressed in the above Note is a return to the earlier frame of mind of the Burney Essay, e.g. p. 20. That essay was full of the thought that Christian evidences are very manifold and largely 'extra-scientific.'—ED.]

---

§ 2. DEFINITION OF TERMS AND PURPOSE OF THIS TREATISE.

[To understand George Romanes' mind close attention must be paid to the following section. Also to the fact, not explicitly noticed by him, that he uses the word 'reason' (here) in a sense closely resembling that in which Mr. Kidd has recently used it in his *Social Evolution.* He uses it, that is, in a restricted sense as equivalent to *the process of scientific ratiocination.* His main position is therefore this: Scientific ratiocination cannot find adequate grounds for belief in God. But the pure agnostic must recognize that God may have revealed Himself by other means than that of scientific ratiocination. As religion is for the whole man, so all human faculties may be required to seek after God and find Him—emotions and experiences of an extra-'rational' kind. The 'pure agnostic' must be prepared to welcome evidence of all sorts.—ED.]

It is desirable to be clear at the outset as to the meaning which I shall throughout attach to certain terms and phrases.

Theism.

It will frequently be said, 'on the theory of Theism,' 'supposing Theism true,' &c. By such phrase my meaning will always be equivalent to—'supposing, for the sake of argument, that the nearest approach which the human mind can make to a true notion of the *ens realissimum*, is that of an inconceivably magnified image of itself at its best.'

Christianity.

Similarly, when it is said, 'supposing Christianity true,' what will be meant is—'supposing for the sake of argument, that the Christian system as a whole, from its earliest dawn in Judaism, to the phase of its development at the present time, is the highest revelation of Himself which a personal Deity has vouchsafed to mankind.' This I intend to signify an attitude of pure agnosticism as regards any particular dogma of Christianity—even that of the Incarnation.

Should it be said that by holding in suspense any distinctive dogma of Christianity, I am not considering Christianity at all, I reply, Not so; I am not writing a theological, but a philosophical treatise, and shall consider Christianity merely as one of many religions, though, of course, the latest, &c. Thus considered, Christianity takes its place as the highest manifestation of evolution in this department of the human mind; but I am not concerned even with so important an ecclesiastical dogma as that of the Incarnation of God in Christ. As far as this treatise has to go, that dogma may or may not be true. The important question for us is, Has God spoken through the medium of our religious instincts? And although this will necessarily involve the question whether or how far in the case of Christianity there is objective evidence of His having spoken by the mouth of holy men [of the Old Testament] which have been since the world began, such will be the case only because it is a question of objective evidence whether or how far the religious instincts of these men, or this race of men, have been so much superior to those of other men, or races of men, as to have enabled them to predict future events of a religious character. And whether or not in these latter days God has spoken by His own Son is not a question for us, further than to investigate the higher class of religious phenomena which unquestionably have been present in the advent and person of Jesus. The question whether Jesus was the Son of God, is, logically speaking, a question of ontology, which, *quâ* pure agnostics, we are logically forbidden to touch.

But elsewhere I ought to show that, from my point of view as to the fundamental question being whether God has spoken at all through the religious instincts of mankind, it may very well be that Christ was not God, and yet that He gave the highest revelation of God. If the 'first Man' was allegorical, why not the 'second'? It is, indeed, an historical fact that the 'second Man' existed, but so likewise may the 'first.' And, as regards the 'personal claims' of Christ, all that He said is not incompatible with His having been Gabriel, and His Holy Ghost, Michael[38]. Or He may have been a man deceived as to His own personality, and yet the vehicle of highest inspiration.

Religion.

By the term 'religion,' I shall mean any theory of personal agency in the universe, belief in which is strong enough in any degree to influence conduct. No term has been used more loosely of late years, or in a greater variety of meanings. Of course anybody may use it in any sense he pleases, provided he defines exactly in what sense he does so. The above seems to be most in accordance with traditional usage.

Agnosticism 'pure' and 'impure'.

The modern and highly convenient term 'Agnosticism,' is used in two very different senses. By its originator, Professor Huxley, it was coined to signify an attitude of reasoned ignorance touching everything that lies beyond the sphere of sense-perception—a professed inability to found valid belief on any other basis. It is in this its original sense—and also, in my opinion, its only philosophically justifiable sense—that I shall understand the term. But the other, and perhaps more popular sense in which the word is now employed, is as the correlative of Mr. H. Spencer's doctrine of the Unknowable.

This latter term is philosophically erroneous, implying important negative knowledge that if there be a God we know this much about Him—that He *cannot* reveal Himself to man[39]. *Pure* agnosticism is as defined by Huxley.

Of all the many scientific men whom I have known, the most pure in his agnosticism—not only in profession but in spirit and conduct—was Darwin. (What he says in his autobiography about Christianity[40] shows no profundity of thought in the direction of philosophy or religion. His mind was too purely inductive for this. But, on this very account, it is the more remarkable that his rejection of Christianity was due, not to any *a priori* bias against the creed on grounds of reason as absurd, but solely on the ground of an apparent moral objection *a posteriori*[41].) Faraday and many other first-rate originators in science were like Darwin.

As an illustration of impure agnosticism take Hume's *a priori* argument against miracles, leading on to the analogous case of the attitude of scientific men towards modern spiritualism. Notwithstanding that they have the close analogy of mesmerism as an object-lesson to warn them, scientific men as a class are here quite as dogmatic as the straightest sect of theologians. I may give examples which can cause no offence, inasmuch as the men in question have themselves made the facts public, viz. —— refusing to go to [a famous spiritualist]; —— refusing to try —— in thought-reading[42]. These men all *professed* to be agnostics at the very time when thus so egregiously violating their philosophy by their conduct.

Of course I do not mean to say that, even to a pure agnostic, reason should not be guided in part by antecedent presumption—e.g. in ordinary life, the *prima facie* case, motive, &c., counts for evidence in a court of law—and where there is a strong antecedent improbability a proportionately greater weight of evidence *a posteriori* is needed to counterbalance it: so that, e.g. better evidence would be needed to convict the Archbishop of Canterbury than a vagabond of pocket-picking. And so it is with speculative philosophy. But in both cases our only guide is known analogy; therefore, the further we are removed from possible experience—i.e. the more remote from experience the sphere contemplated—the less value attaches to antecedent presumptions[43]. *Maximum* remoteness from possible experience is reached in the sphere of the final mystery of things with which religion has to do; so that here all presumption has faded away into a vanishing point, and pure agnosticism is our only rational attitude. In other words, here we should all alike be pure agnostics as far as reason is concerned; and, if any of us are to attain to any information, it can only be by means of some super-added faculty of our minds. The questions as to whether there are any such super-added faculties; if so, whether they ever appear to have been acted upon from without; if they have, in what manner they have; what is their report; how far they are trustworthy in that report, and so on—these are the questions with which this treatise is to be mainly concerned.

My own attitude may be here stated. I do not claim any [religious] certainty of an intuitive kind myself; but am nevertheless able to investigate the abstract logic of the matter. And, although this may seem but barren dialectic, it may, I hope, be of practical service if it secures a fair hearing to the reports given by the vast majority of mankind who unquestionably believe them to emanate from some such super-added faculties—numerous and diverse though their religions be. Besides, in my youth I published an essay (the *Candid Examination*) which excited a good deal of interest at the time, and has been long out of print. In that treatise I have since come to see that I was wrong touching what I constituted the basal argument for my negative conclusion. Therefore I now feel it obligatory on me to publish the following results of my maturer thought, from the same stand-point of pure reason. Even though I have obtained no further light from the side of intuition, I have from that of intellect. So that, if there be in truth any such intuition, I occupy with regard to the organ of it the same position as that of the blind lecturer on optics. But on this very account I cannot be accused of partiality towards it.

It is generally assumed that when a man has clearly perceived agnosticism to be the only legitimate attitude of reason to rest in with regard to religion (as I will subsequently show that it is), he has thereby finished with the matter; he can go no further. The main object of this treatise is to show that such is by no means the case. He has then only begun his enquiry into the grounds and justification of religious belief. For reason is not the only attribute of man, nor is it the only faculty which he habitually employs for the ascertainment of truth. Moral and spiritual faculties are of no less importance in their respective spheres even of everyday life; faith, trust, taste, &c., are as needful in ascertaining truth as to character, beauty, &c., as is reason. Indeed we may take it that reason is concerned in ascertaining truth only where *causation* is concerned; the appropriate organs for its ascertainment where anything else is concerned belong to the moral and spiritual region.

As Herbert Spencer says, 'men of science may be divided into two classes, of which the one, well exemplified by Faraday, keeping their religion and their science absolutely separate, are unperplexed by any incongruities between them, and the other of which, occupying themselves exclusively with the facts of science, never ask what implications they have. Be it trilobite or be it double star, their thought about it is much like the thought of Peter Bell about the primrose[44].' Now, both these classes are logical, since both, as to their religion, adopt an attitude of pure agnosticism, not only in theory, but also in practice. What, however, have we to say of the third class, which Spencer does not mention, although it is, I think, the largest, viz. of those scientific men who expressly abstain from drawing a line of division between science and religion [and then judge of religion purely on the principles and by the method of science[45]]?

There are two opposite casts of mind—the mechanical (scientific, &c.) and the spiritual (artistic, religious, &c.). These may alternate even in the same individual. An 'agnostic' has no hesitation—even though he himself keenly experience the latter—that the former only is worthy of trust. But a *pure* agnostic must know better, as he will perceive that there is nothing to choose between the two in point of trustworthiness. Indeed, if choice has to be made the mystic might claim higher authority for his direct intuitions.

Mr. Herbert Spencer has well said, in the opening section of his Synthetic Philosophy, that wherever human thought appears to be radically divided, [there must be truth on both sides and that the] 'reconciliation' of opposing views is to be found by emphasizing that ultimate element of truth which on each side underlies manifold differences. More than is generally supposed depends on points of view, especially where first principles of a subject are in dispute. Opposite sides of the same shield may present wholly different aspects[46]. Spencer alludes to this with special reference to the conflict between science and religion; and it is in this same connexion that I also allude to it. For it seems to me, after many years of thought upon the subject, that the 'reconciliation' admits of being carried much further than it has been by him. For he effects this reconciliation only to the extent of showing that religion arises from the recognition of fundamental mystery—which it may be proved that science also recognizes in all her fundamental ideas. This, however, is after all little more than a platitude. That our ultimate scientific ideas (i.e. ultimate grounds of experience) are inexplicable, is a proposition which is self-evident since the dawn of human thought. My aim is to carry the 'reconciliation' into much more detail and yet without quitting the grounds of pure reason. I intend to take science and religion in their present highly developed states as such, and show that on a systematic examination of the latter by the methods of the former, the 'conflict' between the two may be not merely 'reconciled' as regards the highest generalities of each, but entirely abolished in all matters of detail which can be regarded as of any great importance.

In any methodical enquiry the first object should be to ascertain the fundamental principles with which the enquiry is concerned. In actual research, however, it is by no means always the case that the enquirer knows, or is able at first to ascertain what those principles are. In fact, it is often only at the end of a research, that they are discovered to be the fundamental principles. Such has been my own experience with regard to the subject of the present enquiry. Although all my thinking life has been concerned, off and on, in contemplating the problem of our religious instincts, the sundry attempts which have been made by mankind for securing their gratification, and the important question as to their objective justification, it is only in advanced years that I have clearly perceived wherein the first principles of such a research must consist. And I doubt whether any one has hitherto clearly defined this point. The principles in question are the nature of causation and the nature of faith.

My objects then in this treatise are, mainly, three: 1st, to purify agnosticism; 2nd, to consider more fully than heretofore, and from the stand-point of pure agnosticism, the nature of natural causation, or, more correctly, the relation of what we know on the subject of such causation to the question of Theism; and, 3rd, again starting from the same stand-point, to consider the religious consciousnesses of men as phenomena of experience (i.e. as regarded by us from without), and especially in their highest phase of development as exhibited in Christianity.

FOOTNOTES:

[38] [I.e. supernatural but not strictly Divine Persons. Surely, however, the proposition is not maintainable.—ED.]

[39] [This is another instance of recurrence to an earlier thought; see Burney Essay, p. 25, and cf. *Mind and Motion and Monism*, p. 117, note 1.—ED.]

[40] *Life and Letters of Charles Darwin*, i. 308.

[41] [See further, here.—ED.]

[42] [On the whole I have thought it best to omit the names.—ED.]

[43] [The MS. note here continues: 'Here introduce all that I say on the subject in my Burney Prize.' I have not, however, introduced any quotation into the text because (1) I think Romanes makes his meaning plain in the text as it stands; (2) I cannot find in the essay in question any exactly appropriate

passage of reasonable length to quote. The greater part of the essay is, however, directed to meet the scientific objection to the doctrine that prayer is answered in the physical region, by showing that this objection consists in an argument from the known to the unknown, i.e. from the known sphere of invariable physical laws to the unknown sphere of God's relation to all such laws; and is, therefore, weak in proportion as the unknown sphere is remote from possible experience of a scientific kind, and admits of an indefinite number of possibilities, more or less conceivable to our imagination, which would or might prevent the scientific argument from having legitimate application to the question in hand.—ED.]

[44] *Fortnightly Review*, Feb. 1894.

[45] [Some such phrase is necessary to complete the sentence.—ED.]

[46] *First Principles*, Part I, ch. 1.

---

§ 3. CAUSALITY.

Only because we are so familiar with the great phenomenon of causality do we take it for granted, and think that we reach an ultimate explanation of anything when we have succeeded in finding the 'cause' thereof: when, in point of fact, we have only succeeded in merging it in the mystery of mysteries. I often wish we could have come into the world, like the young of some other mammals, with all the powers of intellect that we shall ever subsequently attain already developed, but without any individual experience, and so without any of the blunting effects of custom. Could we have done so, surely nothing in the world would more acutely excite our intelligent astonishment than the one universal fact of causation. That everything which happens should have a cause, that this should invariably be proportioned to its effect, so that, no matter how complex the interaction of causes, the same interaction should always produce the same result; that this rigidly exact system of energizing should be found to present all the appearances of universality and of eternity, so that, e.g., the motion of the solar system in space is being determined by some causes beyond human ken, and that we are indebted to billions of cellular unions, each involving billions of separate causes, for our hereditary passage from an invertebrate ancestry,—that such things should be, would surely strike us as the most wonderful fact in this wonderful universe.

Now, although familiarity with this fact has made us forget its wonder to the extent of virtually assuming that we know all about it, philosophical enquiry shows that, besides empirically knowing it to be a fact, we only know one other thing about it, viz.—that our knowledge of it is derived from our own activity when we ourselves are causes. No result of psychological analysis seems to me more certain than this[47]. If it were not for our own volitions, we should be ignorant of what we can now not doubt, on pain of suicidal scepticism, to be the most general fact of nature. Such, at least, seems to me by far the most reasonable theory of our idea of causality, and is the one now most generally entertained by philosophers of every school.

Now, to the plain man it will always seem that if our very notion of causality is derived from our own volition—as our very notion of energy is derived from our sense of effort in overcoming resistance by our volition—presumably the truest notion we can form of that in which causation objectively consists is the notion derived from that known mode of existence which alone gives us the notion of causality at all. Hence the plain man will always infer that all energy is of the nature of will-energy, and all objective causation of the nature of subjective. Nor is this inference confined to the plain man; the deepest philosophical thinkers have arrived at substantially the same opinion, e.g. Hegel, Schopenhauer. So that the direct and most natural interpretation of causality in external nature which is drawn by primitive thought in savages and young children, seems destined to become also the ultimate deliverance of human thought in the highest levels of its culture[48].

But, be this as it may, we are not concerned with any such questions of abstract philosophical speculation. As pure agnostics they lie beyond our sphere. Therefore, I allude to them only for the sake of showing that there is nothing either in the science or philosophy of mankind inimical to the theory of natural causation being the energizing of a will objective to us. And we can plainly see that if such be the case, and if that will be self-consistent, its operations, as revealed in natural causation, must appear to us when considered *en bloc* (or not piece-meal as by savages), non-volitional, or mechanical.

Of all philosophical theories of causality the most repugnant to reason must be those of Hume, Kant and Mill, which while differing from one another agree in this—that they attribute the principle of causality to a creation of our own minds, or in other words deny that there is anything objective in the relation of cause and effect—i.e. in the very thing which all physical science is engaged in discovering in particular cases of it.

The conflict of Science and Religion has always arisen from one common ground of agreement, or fundamental postulate of both parties—without which, indeed, it would plainly have been impossible that any conflict could have arisen, inasmuch as there would then have been no field for battle. Every thesis must rest on some hypothesis; therefore, in cases where two or more rival theses rest on a common hypothesis, the disputes must needs collapse so soon as the common hypothesis is proved erroneous. And proportionably, in whatever degree the previously common hypothesis is shown to be dubious, in that degree are the disputations shown to be possibly unreal. Now, it is one of the main objects of this treatise to show that the common hypothesis on which all the disputes between Science and Religion have arisen, is highly dubious. And not only so, but that quite apart from modern science all the difficulties on the side of intellect (or reason) which religious belief has ever encountered in the past, or can ever encounter in the future, whether in the individual or the race, arise, and arise exclusively, from the self-same ground of this highly dubious hypothesis.

The hypothesis, or fundamental postulate, in question is, *If there be a personal God, He is not immediately concerned with natural causation.* It is assumed that *qua* 'first cause,' He can in no way be concerned with 'second causes,' further than by having started them in the first instance as a great machinery of 'natural causation,' working under 'general laws.' True the theory of Deism, which entertains more or less expressly this hypothesis of 'Deus ex machina,' has during the present century been more and more superseded by that of Theism, which entertains also in some indefinable measure the doctrine of 'immanence'; as well as by that of Pantheism, which expressly holds this doctrine to the exclusion *in toto* of its rival. But Theism has never yet entertained it sufficiently or up to the degree required by the pure logic of the case, while Pantheism has but rarely considered the rival doctrine of personality—or the possible union of immanence with personality.[49]

Now it is the object of this book to go much further than any one has hitherto gone in proving the possibility of this union. For I purpose to show that, provided only we lay aside all prejudice, sentiment, &c., and follow to its logical termination the guidance of pure reason, there are no other conclusions to be reached than these. Namely, (*A*) That if there be a personal God, no reason can be assigned why He should not be immanent in nature, or why all causation should not be the immediate expression of His will. (*B*) That every available reason points to the inference that He probably is so. (*C*) That if He is so, and if His will is self-consistent, all natural causation must needs appear to us 'mechanical.' Therefore (*D*) that it is no argument against the divine origin of a thing, event, &c., to prove it due to natural causation.

After having dealt briefly with (*A*), (*B*) and (*C*), I would show that (*D*) is the most practically important of these four conclusions. For the fundamental hypothesis which I began by mentioning is just the opposite of this. Whether tacitly or expressly, it has always been assumed by both sides in the controversy between Science and Religion, that as soon as this that and the other phenomenon has been explained by means of natural causation, it has thereupon ceased to be ascribable [directly] to God. The distinction between the natural and the supernatural has always been regarded by both sides as indisputably sound, and this fundamental agreement as to ground of battle has furnished the only possible condition to fighting. It has also furnished the condition of all the past, and may possibly furnish the condition of all the future, discomfitures of religion. True religion is indeed learning her lesson that something is wrong in her method of fighting, and many of her soldiers are now waking up to the fact that it is here that her error lies—as in past times they woke up to see the error of denying the movement of the earth, the antiquity of the earth, the origin of species by evolution, &c. But no one, even of her captains and generals, has so far followed up their advantage to its ultimate consequences. And this is what I want to do. The logical advantage is clearly on their side; and it is their own fault if they do not gain the ultimate victory,—not only as against science, but as against intellectual dogmatism in every form. This can be routed all along the line. For science is only the organized study of natural causation, and the experience of every human being, in so far as it leads to dogmatism on purely intellectual grounds, does so on account of entertaining the fundamental postulate in question. The influence of custom and want of imagination is here very great. But the answer always should be to move the ulterior question—what is the nature of natural causation?

Now I propose to push to its full logical conclusion the consequence of this answer. For no one, even the most orthodox, has as yet learnt this lesson of religion to anything like fullness. God is still grudged His own universe, so to speak, as far and as often as He can possibly be. As examples we may take the natural growth of Christianity out of previous religions; the natural spread of it; the natural conversion of St. Paul, or of anybody else. It is still assumed on both sides that there must be something inexplicable or miraculous about a phenomenon in order to its being divine.

What else have science and religion ever had to fight about save on the basis of this common hypothesis, and hence as to whether the causation of such and such a phenomenon has been 'natural' or 'super-natural.' For even the disputes as to science contradicting scripture, ultimately turn on the assumption of inspiration (supposing it genuine) being 'super-natural' as to its causation. Once grant that it is 'natural' and all possible ground of dispute is removed.

I can well understand why infidelity should make the basal assumption in question, because its whole case must rest thereon. But surely it is time for theists to abandon this assumption.

The assumed distinction between causation as natural and super-natural no doubt began in superstition in prehistoric time, and throughout the historical period has continued from a vague feeling that the action of God must be mysterious, and hence that the province of religion must be within the super-sensuous. Now, it is true enough that the finite cannot comprehend the infinite, and hence the feeling in question is logically sound. But under the influence of this feeling, men have always committed the fallacy of concluding that if a phenomenon has been explained in terms of natural causation, it has thereby been explained *in toto*—forgetting that it has only been explained up to the point where such causation is concerned, and that the real question of ultimate causation has merely been thus postponed. And assuredly beyond this point there is an infinitude of mystery sufficient to satisfy the most exacting mystic. For even Herbert Spencer allows that in ultimate analysis all natural causation is inexplicable.

Logically regarded the advance of science, far from having weakened religion, has immeasurably strengthened it. For it has proved the uniformity of natural causation. The so-called natural sphere has increased at the expense of the 'super-natural.' Unquestionably. But although to lower grades of culture this always seems a fact inimical to religion, we may now perceive it is quite the reverse, since it merely goes to abolish the primitive or uncultured distinction in question.

It is indeed most extraordinary how long this distinction has held sway, or how it is the ablest men of all generations have quietly assumed that when once we know the natural causation of any phenomenon, we therefore know all about it—or, as it were, have removed it from the sphere of mystery altogether, when, in point of fact, we have only merged it in a much greater mystery than ever.

But the answer to our astonishment how this distinction has managed to survive so long lies in the extraordinary effect of custom, which here seems to slay reason altogether; and the more a man busies himself with natural causes (e.g. in scientific research) the greater does this slavery to custom become, till at last he seems positively unable to perceive the real state of the case—regarding any rational thinking thereon as chimerical, so that the term 'meta-physical,' even in its etymological sense as super-sensuous or beyond physical causation, becomes a term of rational reproach. Obviously such a man has written himself down, if not an ass, at all events a creature wholly incapable of rationally treating any of the highest problems presented either by nature or by man.

On any logical theory of Theism there can be no such distinction between 'natural' and 'supernatural' as is usually drawn, since on that theory all causation is but the action of the Divine Will. And if we draw any distinction between such action as 'immediate' or 'mediate,' we can only mean this as valid in relation to mankind—i.e. in relation to our experience. For, obviously, it would be wholly incompatible with pure agnosticism to suppose that we are capable of drawing any such distinction in relation to the Divine activity itself. Even apart from the theory of Theism, pure agnosticism must take it that the real distinction is not between natural and supernatural, but between the explicable and the inexplicable—meaning by those terms that which is and that which is not accountable by such causes as fall within the range of human observation. Or, in other words, the distinction is really between the observable and the unobservable causal processes of the universe.

Although science is essentially engaged in explaining, her work is necessarily confined to the sphere of natural causation; beyond that sphere (i.e. the sensuous) she can explain nothing. In other words, even if she were able to explain the natural causation of everything, she would be unable to assign the ultimate *raison d'être* of anything.

It is not my intention to write an essay on the nature of causality, or even to attempt a survey of the sundry theories which have been propounded on this subject by philosophers. Indeed, to attempt this would be little less than to write a history of philosophy itself. Nevertheless it is necessary for my purpose to make a few remarks touching the main branches of thought upon the matter[50].

The remarkable nature of the facts. These are remarkable, since they are common to all human experience. Everything that *happens* has a cause. The same happening has always the same cause—or the same consequent the same antecedent. It is only familiarity with this great fact that prevents universal wonder at it, for, notwithstanding all the theories upon it, no one has ever really shown why it is so. That the same causes always produce the same effects is a proposition which expresses a fundamental fact of our knowledge, but the knowledge of this fact is purely empirical; we can show no reason why it should be a fact. Doubtless, if it were not a fact, there could be no so-called 'Order of Nature,' and consequently no science, no philosophy, or perhaps (if the irregularity were sufficiently frequent) no possibility of human experience. But although this is easy enough to show, it in no wise tends to show why the same causes should always produce the same effects.

So manifest is it that our knowledge of the fact in question is only empirical, that some of our ablest thinkers, such as Hume and Mill, have failed to perceive even so much as the intellectual necessity of looking beyond our empirical knowledge of the fact to gain any explanation of the fact itself. Therefore they give to the world the wholly vacuous, or merely tautological theory of causation—viz. that of constancy of sequence within human observation[51].

If it be said of my argument touching causality, that it is naturalizing or materializing the super-natural or spiritual (as most orthodox persons will feel), my reply is that deeper thought will show it to be at least as susceptible of the opposite view—viz. that it is subsuming the natural into the supernatural, or spiritualizing the material: and a pure agnostic, least of all, should have anything to say as against either of these alternative points of view. Or we may state the matter thus: in as far as pure reason can have anything to say in the matter, she ought to incline towards the view of my doctrine spiritualizing the material, because it is pretty certain that we could know nothing about natural causation—even so much as its existence—but for our own volitions.

Free Will[52].

Having read all that is said to be worth reading on the Free Will controversy, it appears to me that the main issues and their logical conclusions admit of being summed up in a very few words, thus:—

1. A writer, before he undertakes to deal with this subject at all, should be conscious of fully perceiving the fundamental distinction between responsibility as merely legal and as also moral; otherwise he cannot but miss the very essence of the question in debate. No one questions the patent fact of responsibility as legal; the only question is touching responsibility as moral. Yet the principal bulk of literature on Free Will and Necessity arises from disputants on both sides failing to perceive this basal distinction. Even such able writers as Spencer, Huxley and Clifford are in this position.

2. The root question is as to whether the will is caused or un-caused. For however much this root-question may be obscured by its own abundant foliage, the latter can have no existence but that which it derives from the former.

3. Consequently, if libertarians grant causality as appertaining to the will, however much they may beat about the bush, they are surrendering their position all along the line, unless they fall back upon the more ultimate question as to the nature of natural causation. Now it can be proved that this more ultimate question is [scientifically] unanswerable. Therefore both sides may denominate natural causation *x*—an unknown quantity.

4. Hence the whole controversy ought to be seen by both sides to resolve itself into this—is or is not the will determined by *x*? And, if this seems but a barren question to debate, I do not undertake to deny the fact. At the same time there is clearly this real issue remaining—viz. Is the will self-determining, or is it determined—i.e. *from without*?

5. If determined from without, is there any room for freedom, in the sense required for saving the doctrine of moral responsibility? And I think the answer to this must be an unconditional negative.

6. But, observe, it is not one and the same thing to ask, Is the will entirely determined from without? and Is the will entirely determined by natural

causation (x)? For the unknown quantity x may very well include x', if by x' we understand all the unknown ingredients of personality.

7. Hence, determinists gain no advantage over their adversaries by any possible proof (at present impossible) that all acts of will are due to natural causation, unless they can show the nature of the latter, and that it is of such a nature as supports their conclusion. For aught we at present know, the will may very well be free in the sense required, even though all its acts are due to x.

8. In particular, for aught we know to the contrary, all may be due to x', i.e. all causation may be of the nature of will (as, indeed, many systems of philosophy maintain), with the result that every human will is of the nature of a First Cause. In support of which possibility it may be remarked that most philosophies are led to the theory of a *causa causarum* as regards x.

9. To the obvious objection that with a plurality of first causes—each the *fons et origo* of a new and never-ending stream of causality—the cosmos must sooner or later become a chaos by cumulative intersection of the streams, the answer is to be found in the theory of monism[53].

10. Nevertheless, the ultimate difficulty remains which is depicted in my essay on the 'World as an Eject[54].' But this, again, is merged in the mystery of Personality, which is only known as an inexplicable, and seemingly ultimate, fact.

11. So that the general conclusion of the whole matter must be—pure agnosticism.

FOOTNOTES:

[47] [Here it was intended to insert further explanation 'showing that mere observation of causality in external nature would not have yielded idea of anything further than time and space relations.'—ED.]

[48] [This theory was suggested in the Burney Essay, p. 136, and ridiculed in the *Candid Examination*; see here. Romanes intended at this point to consider at greater length his old views 'on causation as due to being *qua* being.'—ED.]

[49] See, however, Aubrey Moore in *Lux Mundi*, pp. 94-96, and Le Conte, *Evolution in its Relation to Religious Thought*, pp. 335, ff. [N.B. The references not enclosed in brackets are the author's, not mine.—ED.]

[50] [Nothing more however was written than what follows immediately.—ED.]

[51] [The author intended further to show the vacuity of this theory and point out how Mill himself appears to perceive it by his introduction after the term

'invariably' of the term 'unconditionally'; he refers also to Martineau, *Study of Religion*, i. pp. 152, 3.—ED.]

[52] [Romanes' thoughts about Free Will are more lucidly expressed in an essay published subsequently to these Notes in *Mind and Motion and Monism*, pp. 129 ff.—ED.]

[53] [See here.—ED.]

[54] *Contemporary Review*, July 1886. [But the 'ultimate difficulty' referred to above would seem to be the relation of manifold dependent human wills to the One Ultimate and All-embracing Will.—ED.]

---

§ 4. FAITH.

Faith in its religious sense is distinguished not only from opinion (or belief founded on reason alone), in that it contains a spiritual element: it is further distinguished from belief founded on the affections, by needing an active co-operation of the will. Thus all parts of the human mind have to be involved in faith—intellect, emotions, will. We 'believe' in the theory of evolution on grounds of reason alone; we 'believe' in the affection of our parents, children, &c., almost (or it may be exclusively) on what I have called spiritual grounds—i.e. on grounds of spiritual experience; for this we need no exercise either of reason or of will. But no one can 'believe' in God, or *a fortiori* in Christ, without also a severe effort of will. This I hold to be a matter of fact, whether or not there be a God or a Christ.

Observe will is to be distinguished from desire. It matters not what psychologists may have to say upon this subject. Whether desire differs from will in kind or only in degree—whether will is desire in action, so to speak, and desire but incipient will—are questions with which we need not trouble ourselves. For it is certain that there are agnostics who would greatly prefer being theists, and theists who would give all they possess to be Christians, if they could thus secure promotion by purchase—i.e. by one single act of will. But yet the desire is not strong enough to sustain the will in perpetual action, so as to make the continual sacrifices which Christianity entails. Perhaps the hardest of these sacrifices to an intelligent man is that of his own intellect. At least I am certain that this is so in my own case. I have been so long accustomed to constitute my reason my sole judge of truth, that even while reason itself tells me it is not unreasonable to expect that the heart and the will should be required to join with reason in seeking God (for religion is for the *whole* man), I am too jealous of my reason to exercise my will in the direction of my most heart-felt desires. For assuredly the strongest desire of my nature is to find that that nature is not deceived in its highest aspirations. Yet I cannot bring myself so much as to make a venture in the direction of faith. For instance, regarded from one point of view it seems reasonable enough that Christianity should have enjoined the *doing* of the doctrine as a necessary condition to ascertaining (i.e. 'believing') its truth. But from another, and my more habitual point of view, it seems almost an affront to reason to make any such 'fool's experiment'—just as to some scientific men it seems absurd and childish to expect them to investigate the 'superstitious' follies of modern spiritualism. Even the simplest act of will in regard to religion—that of prayer—has not been performed by me for at least a quarter of a century, simply because it has seemed so impossible to pray, as it were, hypothetically, that much as I have always desired to be able to pray, I cannot will the attempt. To justify myself for what my better judgement has often seen to be essentially irrational, I have ever made sundry excuses. The chief of them has run thus. Even supposing Christianity true, and even supposing that after having so far sacrificed my reason to my desire as to have satisfied the supposed conditions to obtaining 'grace,' or direct illumination from God,—even then would not my reason turn round and revenge herself upon me? For surely even then my habitual scepticism would make me say to myself—'this is all very sublime and very comforting; but what evidence have you to give me that the whole business is anything more than self-delusion? The wish was probably father to the thought, and you might much better have performed your "act of will" by going in for a course of Indian hemp.' Of course a Christian would answer to this that the internal light would not admit of such doubt, any more than seeing the sun does—that God knows us well enough to prevent that, &c., and also that it is unreasonable not to try an experiment lest the result should prove too good to be credible, and so on. And I do not dispute that the Christian would be justified in so answering, but I only adduce the matter as an illustration of the difficulty which is experienced in conforming to all the conditions of attaining to Christian faith—even supposing it to be sound. Others have doubtless other difficulties, but mine is chiefly, I think, that of an undue regard to reason, as against heart and will—undue, I mean, if so it be that Christianity is true, and the conditions to faith in it have been of divine ordination.

This influence of will on belief, even in matters secular, is the more pronounced the further removed these matters may be from demonstration (as already remarked); but this is most of all the case where our personal interests are affected—whether these be material or intellectual, such as credit for consistency, &c. See, for example, how closely, in the respects we are considering, political beliefs resemble religious. Unless the points of difference are such that truth is virtually demonstrable on one side, so that adhesion to the opposite is due to *conscious* sacrifice of integrity to expediency, we always find that party-spectacles so colour the view as to leave reason at the mercy of will, custom, interest, and all the other circumstances which similarly operate on religious beliefs. It seems to make but little difference in either case what level of general education, mental power, special training, &c., is brought to bear upon the question under judgement. From the Premier to the peasant we find the same difference of opinion in politics as we do in religion. And in each case the explanation is the same. Beliefs are so little dependent on reason alone that in such regions of thought—i.e. where personal interests are affected and the evidences of truth are not in their nature demonstrable—it really seems as if reason ceases to be a judge of evidence or guide to truth, and becomes a mere advocate of opinion already formed on quite other grounds. Now these other grounds are, as we have seen, mainly the accidents of habit or custom, wish being father to the thought, &c.

Now this may be all deplorable enough in politics, and in all other beliefs secular; but who shall say it is not exactly as it ought to be in the matter of beliefs religious? For, unless we beg the question of a future life in the negative, we must entertain at least the possibility of our being in a state of probation in respect of an honest use not only of our reason, but probably still more of those other ingredients of human nature which go to determine our beliefs touching this most important of all matters.

It is remarkable how even in politics it is the moral and spiritual elements of character which lead to success in the long run, even more than intellectual ability—supposing, of course, that the latter is not below the somewhat high level of our Parliamentary assemblies.

As regards the part that is played by will in the determining of belief, one can show how unconsciously large this is even in matters of secular interest. Reason is very far indeed from being the sole guide of judgement that it is usually taken to be—so far, indeed, that, save in matters approaching downright demonstration (where of course there is no room for any other ingredient) it is usually hampered by custom, prejudice, dislike, &c., to a degree that would astonish the most sober philosopher could he lay bare to himself all the mental processes whereby the complex act of assent or dissent is eventually determined[55].

As showing how little reason alone has to do with the determining of religious belief, let us take the case of mathematicians. This I think is the fairest case we can take, seeing that of all intellectual pursuits that of mathematical research is the most exact, as well as the most exclusive in its demand upon the powers of reason, and hence that, as a class, the men who have achieved highest eminence in that pursuit may be fairly taken as the fittest representatives of our species in respect of the faculty of pure reason. Yet whenever they have turned their exceptional powers in this respect upon the problems of religion, how suggestively well balanced are their opposite conclusions—so much so indeed that we can only conclude that reason counts for very little in the complex of mental processes which here determine judgement.

Thus, if we look to the greatest mathematicians in the world's history, we find Kepler and Newton as Christians; La Place, on the other hand, an infidel. Or, coming to our own times, and confining our attention to the principal seat of mathematical study:—when I was at Cambridge, there was a galaxy of genius in that department emanating from that place such as had never before been equalled. And the curious thing in our present connexion is that all the most illustrious names were ranged on the side of orthodoxy. Sir W. Thomson, Sir George Stokes, Professors Tait, Adams, Clerk-Maxwell, and Cayley—not to mention a number of lesser lights, such as Routh, Todhunter, Ferrers, &c.—were all avowed Christians. Clifford had only just moved at a bound from the extreme of asceticism to that of infidelity—an individual instance which I deem of particular interest in the present connexion, as showing the dominating influence of a forcedly emotional character even on so powerful an intellectual one, for the *rationality* of the whole structure of Christian belief cannot have so reversed its poles within a few months.

Now it would doubtless be easy to find elsewhere than in Cambridge mathematicians of the first order who in our own generation are, or have been, professedly anti-Christian in their beliefs,—although certainly not so great an array of such extraordinary powers. But, be this as it may, the case of Cambridge in my own time seems to me of itself enough to prove that Christian belief is neither made nor marred by the highest powers of reasoning, apart from other and still more potent factors.

Faith and Superstition.

Whether or not Christianity is true, there is a great distinction between these two things. For while the main ingredient of Christian faith is the moral element, this has no part in superstition. In point of fact, the only point of resemblance is that both present the mental state called *belief*. It is on this account they are so often confounded by anti-Christians, and even by non-Christians; the much more important point of difference is not noted, viz. that belief in the one case is purely intellectual, while in the other it is chiefly moral. *Qua* purely intellectual, belief may indicate nothing but sheer credulity in absence of evidence; but where a moral basis is added, the case is clearly different; for even if it appears to be sheer credulity to an outsider, that may be because he does not take into account the additional evidence supplied by the moral facts.

Faith and superstition are often confounded, or even identified. And, unquestionably, they are identical up to a certain point—viz. they both present the mental state of *belief*. All people can see this; but not all people can see further, or define the *differentiae*. These are as follows: First, supposing

Christianity true, there is the spiritual verification. Second, supposing Christianity false, there is still the moral ingredient, which *ex hypothesi* is absent in superstition. In other words, both faith and superstition rest on an intellectual basis (which may be pure credulity); but faith rests also on a moral, even if not likewise on a spiritual. Even in human relations there is a wide difference between 'belief' in a scientific theory and 'faith' in a personal character. And the difference is in the latter comprising a moral element.

'Faith-healing,' therefore, has no real point of resemblance with 'thy faith hath saved thee' of the New Testament, unless we sink the personal differences between a modern faith-healer and Jesus Christ as objects of faith.

Belief is not exclusively founded on objective evidence appealing to reason (opinion), but mainly on subjective evidence appealing to some altogether different faculty (faith). Now, whether Christians are right or wrong in what they believe, I hold it as certain as anything can be that the distinction which I have just drawn, and which they all implicitly draw for themselves, is logically valid. For no one is entitled to deny the possibility of what may be termed an organ of spiritual discernment. In fact to do so would be to vacate the position of pure agnosticism *in toto*—and this even if there were no objective, or strictly scientific, evidences in favour of such an organ, such as we have in the lives of the saints, and, in a lower degree, in the universality of the religious sentiment. Now, if there be such an organ, it follows from preceding paragraphs, that not only will the main evidences for Christianity be subjective, but that they ought to be so: they ought to be so, I mean, on the Christian supposition of the object of Christianity being moral probation, and 'faith' both the test and the reward.

From this many practical considerations ensue. E.g. the duty of parents to educate their children in what they *believe* as distinguished from what they *know*. This would be unjustifiable if faith were the same as opinion. But it is fully justifiable if a man not only knows that he believes (opinion) but believes that he knows (faith). Whether or not the Christian differs from the 'natural man' in having a spiritual organ of cognition, provided he honestly believes such is the case, it would be immoral in him not to proceed in accordance with what he thus believes to be his knowledge. This obligation is recognized in education in every other case. He is morally right even if mentally deluded.

Huxley, in *Lay Sermons*, says that faith has been proved a 'cardinal sin' by science. Now, this is true enough of credulity, superstition, &c., and science has done no end of good in developing our ideas of method, evidence, &c. But this is all on the side of intellect. 'Faith' is not touched by such facts or considerations. And what a terrible hell science would have made of the world, if she had abolished the 'spirit of faith' even in human relations. The fact is, Huxley falls into the common error of identifying 'faith' with opinion.

Supposing Christianity true, it is very reasonable that faith in the sense already explained should be constituted the test of divine acceptance. If there be such a thing as Christ's winnowing fan, the quality of sterling weight for the discovery of which it is adapted cannot be conceived as anything other than this moral quality. No one could suppose a revelation appealing to the mere intellect of man, since acceptance would thus become a mere matter of prudence in subscribing to a demonstration made by higher intellects.

It is also a matter of fact that if Christianity is truthful in representing this world as a school of moral probation, we cannot conceive a system better adapted to this end than is the world, or a better schoolmaster than Christianity. This is proved not only by general reasoning, but also by the work of Christianity in the world, its adaptation to individual needs, &c. Consider also the extraordinary diversity of human characters in respect both of morality and spirituality though all are living in the same world. Out of the same external material or environment such astonishingly diverse products arise according to the use made of it. Even human suffering in its worst forms can be welcome if justified by faith in such an object. 'Ills have no weight, and tears no bitterness,' but are rather to be 'gloried in[56].'

It is a further fact that only by means of this theory of probation is it possible to give any meaning to the world, i.e. any *raison d'être* of human existence.

Supposing Christianity true, every man must stand or fall by the results of his own conduct, as developed through his own moral character. (This could not be so if the test were intellectual ability.) Yet this does not hinder that the exercise of will in the direction of religion should need help in order to attain belief. Nor does it hinder that some men should need more help and others less. Indeed, it may well be that some men are intentionally precluded from receiving any help, so as not to increase their responsibility, or receive but little, so as to constitute intellectual difficulties a moral trial. But clearly, if such things are so, we are inadequate judges.

It is a fact that we all feel the intellectual part of man to be 'higher' than the animal, whatever our theory of his origin. It is a fact that we all feel the moral part of man to be 'higher' than the intellectual, whatever our theory of either may be. It is also a fact that we all similarly feel the spiritual to be 'higher' than the moral, whatever our theory of religion may be. It is what we understand by man's moral, and still more his spiritual, qualities that go to constitute 'character.' And it is astonishing how in all walks of life it is character that tells in the long run.

It is a fact that these distinctions are all well marked and universally recognized—viz.

{Animality.

{Intellectuality.

Human {Morality.

{Spirituality.

Morality and spirituality are to be distinguished as two very different things. A man may be highly moral in his conduct without being in any degree spiritual in his nature, and, though to a lesser extent, vice versa. And, objectively, we see the same distinction between morals and religion. By spirituality I mean the religious temperament, whether or not associated with any particular creed or dogma.

There is no doubt that intellectual pleasures are more satisfying and enduring than sensual—or even sensuous. And, to those who have experienced them, so it is with spiritual over intellectual, artistic, &c. This is an objective fact, abundantly testified to by every one who has had experience: and it seems to indicate that the spiritual nature of man is the highest part of man—the [culminating] point of his being.

It is probably true, as Renan says in his posthumous work, that there will always be materialists and spiritualists, inasmuch as it will always be observable on the one hand that there is no thought without brain, while, on the other hand, instincts of man will always aspire to higher beliefs. But this is just what ought to be if religion is true, and we are in a state of probation. And is it not probable that the materialistic position (discredited even by philosophy) is due simply to custom and want of imagination? Else why the inextinguishable instincts?

It is much more easy to disbelieve than to believe. This is obvious on the side of reason, but it is also true on that of spirit, for to disbelieve is in accordance with environment or custom, while to believe necessitates a spiritual use of the imagination. For both these reasons, very few unbelievers have any justification, either intellectual or spiritual, for their own unbelief.

Unbelief is usually due to indolence, often to prejudice, and never a thing to be proud of.

'Why should it be thought a thing incredible with you that God should raise the dead?' Clearly no answer can be given by the pure agnostic. But he will naturally say in reply, 'the question rather is, why should it be thought credible with you that there is a God, or, if there is, that he should raise the dead?'

And I think the wise Christian will answer, 'I believe in the resurrection of the dead, partly on grounds of reason, partly on those of intuition, but chiefly on both combined; so to speak, it is my whole character which accepts the whole system of which the doctrine of personal immortality forms an essential part.' And to this it may be fairly added that the Christian doctrine of the resurrection of our bodily form cannot have been arrived at for the purpose of meeting modern materialistic objections to the doctrine of personal immortality; hence it is certainly a strange doctrine to have been propounded at that time, together with its companion, and scarcely less distinctive, doctrine of the vileness of the body. Why was it not said that the 'soul' alone should survive as a disembodied 'spirit'? Or if form were supposed necessary for man as distinguished from God, that he was to be an angel? But, be this as it may, the doctrine of the resurrection seems to have fully met beforehand the materialistic objection to a future life, and so to have raised the ulterior question with which this paragraph opens.

We have seen in the Introduction that all first principles even of scientific facts are known by intuition and not by reason. No one can deny this. Now, if there be a God, the fact is certainly of the nature of a first principle; for it must be the first of all first principles. No one can dispute this. No one can therefore dispute the necessary conclusion, that, if there be a God, He is knowable, (if knowable at all) by intuition and not by reason.

Indeed a little thought is enough to show that from its very nature as such, reason must be incapable of adjudicating on the subject, for it is a process of inferring from the known to the unknown.

Or thus. It would be against reason itself to suppose that God, even if He exists, can be known by reason; He must be known, if knowable at all, by intuition[57].

Observe, although God might give an objective revelation of Himself, e.g. as Christians believe He has, even this would not give knowledge of Him save to those who believe the revelations genuine; and I doubt whether it is logically possible for any form of objective revelation of itself to compel belief in it. Assuredly one rising from the dead to testify thereto would not, nor would letters of fire across the sky do so. But, even if it were logically possible, we need not consider the abstract possibility, seeing that, as a matter of fact, no such demonstrative revelation has been given.

Hence, the only legitimate attitude of pure reason is pure agnosticism. No one can deny this. But, it will be said, there is this vast difference between our intuitive knowledge of all other first principles and that alleged of the 'first of all first principles,' viz. that the latter is confessedly *not* known to all men. Now, assuredly, there is here a vast difference. But so there ought to be, if we are here in a state of probation, as before explained. And that we are in such a state is not only the hypothesis of religion, but the sole rational explanation as well as moral justification of our existence as rational beings and moral agents[58].

It is not necessarily true, as J.S. Mill and all other agnostics think, that even if internal intuition be of divine origin, the illumination thus furnished can only be of evidential value to the individual subject thereof. On the contrary, it may be studied objectively, even if not experienced subjectively; and ought to be so studied by a pure agnostic desirous of light from any quarter. Even if he does not know it as a noumenon he can investigate it as a phenomenon. And, supposing it to be of divine origin, as its subjects believe and he has no reason to doubt, he may gain much evidence against its being a mere psychological illusion from identical reports of it in all ages. Thus, if any large section of the race were to see flames issuing from magnets, there would be no doubt as to their objective reality.

The testimony given by Socrates to the occurrence in himself of an internal Voice, having all the definiteness of an auditory hallucination, has given rise to much speculation by subsequent philosophers.

Many explanations are suggested, but if we remember the critical nature of Socrates' own mind, the literal nature of his mode of teaching, and the high authority which attaches to Plato's opinion on the subject, the probability seems to incline towards the 'Demon' having been, in Socrates' own consciousness, an actual auditory sensation. Be this however as it may, I suppose there is no question that we may adopt this view of the matter at least to the extent of classifying Socrates with Luther, Pascal, &c., not to mention all the line of Hebrew and other prophets, who agree in speaking of a Divine Voice.

If so, the further question arises whether we are to classify all these with lunatics in whom the phenomena of auditory hallucination are habitual.

Without doubt this hypothesis is most in accordance with the temper of our age, partly because it obeys the law of parsimony, and partly because it [negatives] *a priori* the possibility of revelation.

But if we look at the matter from the point of view of pure agnosticism, we are not entitled to adopt so rough and ready an interpretation.

Suppose then that not only Socrates and all great religious reformers and founders of religious systems both before and after him were similarly stricken with mental disease, but that similar phenomena had occurred in the case of all scientific discoverers such as Galileo, Newton, Darwin, &c.— supposing all these men to have declared that their main ideas had been communicated by subjective sensations as of spoken language, so that all the progress of the world's scientific thought had resembled that of the world's religious thought, and had been attributed by the promoters thereof to direct inspirations of this kind—would it be possible to deny that the testimony thus afforded to the fact of subjective revelation would have been overwhelming? Or could it any longer have been maintained that supposing a revelation to be communicated subjectively the fact thereof could only be of any evidential value to the recipient himself? To this it will no doubt be answered, 'No, but in the case supposed the evidence arises not from the fact of their subjective intuition but from that of its objective verification in the results of science.' Quite so; but this is exactly the test appealed to by the Hebrew prophets—the test of true and lying prophets being in the fulfilment or non-fulfilment of their prophecies and 'By their fruits ye shall know them.'

Therefore it is as absurd to say that the religious consciousness of minds other than our own can be barred antecedently as evidence, as it is to say that testimony to the miraculous is similarly barred. The pure agnostic must always carefully avoid the 'high *priori* road.' But, on the other hand, he must be all the more assiduous in estimating fairly the character, both as to quantity and quality, of evidence *a posteriori*. Now this evidence in the present case is twofold, positive and negative. It will be convenient to consider the negative first.

The negative evidence is furnished by the nature of man without God. It is thoroughly miserable, as is well shown by Pascal, who has devoted the whole of the first part of his treatise to this subject. I need not go over the ground which he has already so well traversed.

Some men are not conscious of the cause of this misery: this, however, does not prevent the fact of their being miserable. For the most part they conceal the fact as well as possible from themselves, by occupying their minds with society, sport, frivolity of all kinds, or, if intellectually disposed, with science, art, literature, business, &c. This however is but to fill the starving belly with husks. I know from experience the intellectual distractions of scientific research, philosophical speculation, and artistic pleasures; but am also well aware that even when all are taken together and well sweetened to taste, in respect of consequent reputation, means, social position, &c., the whole concoction is but as high confectionery to a starving man. He may cheat himself for a time—especially if he be a strong man—into the belief that he is nourishing himself by denying his natural appetite; but soon finds he was made for some altogether different kind of food, even though of much less tastefulness as far as the palate is concerned.

Some men indeed never acknowledge this articulately or distinctly even to themselves, yet always show it plainly enough to others. Take, e.g., 'that last infirmity of noble minds.' I suppose the most exalted and least 'carnal' of worldly joys consists in the adequate recognition by the world of high achievement by ourselves. Yet it is notorious that—

"It is by God decreed

Fame shall not satisfy the highest need."

It has been my lot to know not a few of the famous men of our generation, and I have always observed that this is profoundly true. Like all other 'moral' satisfactions, this soon palls by custom, and as soon as one end of distinction is reached, another is pined for. There is no finality to rest in, while disease and death are always standing in the background. Custom may even blind men to their own misery, so far as not to make them realize what is wanting; yet the want is there.

I take it then as unquestionably true that this whole negative side of the subject proves a vacuum in the soul of man which nothing can fill save faith in God.

Now take the positive side. Consider the happiness of religious—and chiefly of the highest religious, i.e. Christian—belief. It is a matter of fact that besides being most intense, it is most enduring, growing, and never staled by custom. In short, according to the universal testimony of those who have it, it differs from all other happiness not only in degree but in kind. Those who have it can usually testify to what they used to be without it. It has no relation to intellectual status. It is a thing by itself and supreme.

So much for the individual. But positive evidence does not end here. Look at the effects of Christian belief as exercised on human society—1st, by individual Christians on the family, &c.; and, 2nd, by the Christian Church on the world.

All this may lead on to an argument from the adaptation of Christianity to human higher needs. All men must feel these needs more or less in proportion as their higher natures, moral and spiritual, are developed. Now Christianity is the only religion which is adapted to meet them, and, according to those who are alone able to testify, does so most abundantly. All these men, of every sect, nationality, &c., agree in their account of their subjective experience; so as to this there can be no question. The only question is as to whether they are all deceived.

PEU DE CHOSE.

'La vie est vaine:

Un peu d'amour,

Un peu de haine ...

Et puis—bon jour!

La vie est brève:

Un peu d'espoir,

Un peu de rêve ...

Et puis—bon soir!'

The above is a terse and true criticism of this life without hope of a future one. Is it satisfactory? But Christian faith, as a matter of fact, changes it entirely.

'The night has a thousand eyes,

And the day but one;

Yet the light of a whole world dies

With the setting sun.

The mind has a thousand eyes,

And the heart but one;

Yet the light of a whole life dies

When love is done.'

Love is known to be all this. How great, then, is Christianity, as being the religion of love, and causing men to believe both in the cause of love's supremacy and the infinity of God's love to man.

FOOTNOTES:

[55] Cf. Pascal, *Pensées*. 'For we must not mistake ourselves, we have as much that is automatic in us as intellectual, and hence it comes that the instrument by which persuasion is brought about is not demonstration alone. How few things are demonstrated! Proofs can only convince the mind; custom makes our strongest proofs and those which we hold most firmly, it sways the automaton, which draws the unconscious intellect after it.... It is then custom that makes so many men Christians, custom that makes them Turks, heathen, artisans, soldiers, &c. Lastly, we must resort to custom when once the mind has seen where truth is, in order to slake our thirst and steep ourselves in that belief which escapes us at every hour, for to have proofs always at hand were too onerous. We must acquire a more easy belief, that of custom, which

without violence, without art, without argument, causes our assent and inclines all our powers to this belief, so that our soul naturally falls into it....

'It is not enough to believe only by force of conviction if the automaton is inclined to believe the contrary. Both parts of us then must be obliged to believe, the intellect by arguments which it is enough to have admitted once in our lives, the automaton by custom, and by not allowing it to incline in the contrary direction. *Inclina cor meum Deus.*' See also Newman's *Grammar of Assent*, chap. vi. and Church's *Human Life and its Conditions*, pp. 67-9.

[56] [The author has added, "For suffering in brutes see further on," but nothing further on the subject appears to have been written.—ED.]

[57] [In this connexion I may again notice that two days before his death George Romanes expressed his cordial approval of Professor Knight's *Aspects of Theism*—a work in which great stress is laid on the argument from intuition in different forms.—ED.]

[58] On this subject see Pascal, *Pensées* (Kegan Paul's trans.) p. 103.

---

§ 5. FAITH IN CHRISTIANITY.

Christianity comes up for serious investigation in the present treatise, because this *Examination of Religion* [i.e. of the validity of the religious consciousness] has to do with the evidences of Theism presented by man, and not only by nature *minus* man. Now of the religious consciousness Christianity is unquestionably the highest product.

When I wrote the preceding treatise [the *Candid Examination*], I did not sufficiently appreciate the immense importance of *human* nature, as distinguished from physical nature, in any enquiry touching Theism. But since then I have seriously studied anthropology (including the science of comparative religions), psychology and metaphysics, with the result of clearly seeing that human nature is the most important part of nature as a whole whereby to investigate the theory of Theism. This I ought to have anticipated on merely *a priori* grounds, and no doubt should have perceived, had I not been too much immersed in merely physical research.

Moreover, in those days, I took it for granted that Christianity was played out, and never considered it at all as having any rational bearing on the question of Theism. And, though this was doubtless inexcusable, I still think that the rational standing of Christianity has materially improved since then. For then it seemed that Christianity was destined to succumb as a rational system before the double assault of Darwin from without and the negative school of criticism from within. Not only the book of organic nature, but likewise its own sacred documents, seemed to be declaring against it. But now all this has been very materially changed. We have all more or less grown to see that Darwinism is like Copernicanism, &c., in this respect[59]; while the outcome of the great textual battle[60] is impartially considered a signal victory for Christianity. Prior to the new [Biblical] science, there was really no rational basis in thoughtful minds, either for the date of any one of the New Testament books, or, consequently, for the historical truth of any one of the events narrated in them. Gospels, Acts and Epistles were all alike shrouded in this uncertainty. Hence the validity of the eighteenth-century scepticism. But now all this kind of scepticism has been rendered obsolete, and for ever impossible; while the certainty of enough of St. Paul's writings for the practical purpose of displaying the belief of the apostles has been established, as well as the certainty of the publication of the Synoptics within the first century. An enormous gain has thus accrued to the objective evidences of Christianity. It is most important that the expert investigator should be exact, and, as in any other science, the lay public must take on authority as trustworthy only what both sides are agreed upon. But, as in any other science, experts are apt to lose sight of the importance of the main results agreed upon, in their fighting over lesser points still in dispute. Now it is enough for us that the Epistles to the Romans, Galatians, and Corinthians, have been agreed upon as genuine, and that the same is true of the Synoptics so far as concerns the main doctrine of Christ Himself.

The extraordinary candour of Christ's biographers must not be forgotten[61]. Notice also such sentences as 'but some doubted,' and (in the account of Pentecost) 'these men are full of new wine[62].' Such observations are wonderfully true to human nature; but no less wonderfully opposed to any 'accretion' theory.

Observe, when we become honestly pure agnostics the whole scene changes by the change in our point of view. We may then read the records impartially, or on their own merits, without any antecedent conviction that they must be false. It is then an open question whether they are not true as history.

There is so much to be said in objective evidence for Christianity that were the central doctrines thus testified to anything short of miraculous, no one would doubt. But we are not competent judges *a priori* of what a revelation should be. If our agnosticism be *pure*, we have no right to pre-judge the case on *prima facie* grounds.

One of the strongest pieces of objective evidence in favour of Christianity is not sufficiently enforced by apologists. Indeed, I am not aware that I have ever seen it mentioned. It is the absence from the biography of Christ of any doctrines which the subsequent growth of human knowledge—whether in natural science, ethics, political economy, or elsewhere—has had to discount. This negative argument is really almost as strong as is the positive one from what Christ did teach. For when we consider what a large number of sayings are recorded of—or at least attributed to—Him, it becomes most remarkable that in literal truth there is no reason why any of His words should ever pass away in the sense of becoming obsolete. 'Not even now could it be easy,' says John Stuart Mill, 'even for an unbeliever, to find a better translation of the rule of virtue from the abstract into the concrete, than to endeavour so to live that Christ would approve our life[63].' Contrast Jesus Christ in this respect with other thinkers of like antiquity. Even Plato, who, though some 400 years B.C. in point of time, was greatly in advance of Him in respect of philosophic thought—not only because Athens then presented the extraordinary phenomenon which it did of genius in all directions never since equalled, but also because he, following Socrates, was, so to speak, the greatest representative of human reason in the direction of spirituality—even Plato, I say, is nowhere in this respect as compared with Christ. Read the dialogues, and see how enormous is the contrast with the Gospels in respect of errors of all kinds—reaching even to absurdity in respect of reason, and to sayings shocking to the moral sense. Yet this is confessedly the highest level of human reason on the lines of spirituality, when unaided by alleged revelation.

Two things may be said in reply. First, that the Jews (Rabbis) of Christ's period had enunciated most of Christ's ethical sayings. But, even so far as this is true, the sayings were confessedly extracted or deduced from the Old Testament, and so *ex hypothesi* due to original inspiration. Again, it is not very far true, because, as *Ecce Homo* says, the ethical sayings of Christ, even when anticipated by Rabbis and the Old Testament, were *selected* by Him.

It is a general, if not a universal, rule that those who reject Christianity with contempt are those who care not for religion of any kind. 'Depart from us' has always been the sentiment of such. On the other hand, those in whom the religious sentiment is intact, but who have rejected Christianity on intellectual grounds, still almost deify Christ. These facts are remarkable.

If we estimate the greatness of a man by the influence which he has exerted on mankind, there can be no question, even from the secular point of view, that Christ is much the greatest man who has ever lived.

It is on all sides worth considering (blatant ignorance or base vulgarity alone excepted) that the revolution effected by Christianity in human life is immeasurable and unparalleled by any other movement in history; though most nearly approached by that of the Jewish religion, of which, however, it is a development, so that it may be regarded as of a piece with it. If thus regarded, this whole system of religion is so immeasurably in advance of all others, that it may fairly be said, if it had not been for the Jews, the human race would not have had any religion worth our serious attention as such.

The whole of that side of human nature would never have been developed in civilized life. And although there are numberless individuals who are not conscious of its development in themselves, yet even these have been influenced to an enormous extent by the atmosphere of religion around them.

But not only is Christianity thus so immeasurably in advance of all other religions. It is no less so of every other system of thought that has ever been promulgated in regard to all that is moral and spiritual. Whether it be true or false, it is certain that neither philosophy, science, nor poetry has ever produced results in thought, conduct, or beauty in any degree to be compared with it. This I think will be on all hands allowed as regards conduct. As regards thought and beauty it may be disputed. But, consider, what has all the science or all the philosophy of the world done for the thought of mankind to be compared with the one doctrine, 'God is love'? Whether or not true, conceive what belief in it has been to thousands of millions of our race—i.e. its influence on human thought, and thence on human conduct. Thus to admit its incomparable influence in conduct is indirectly to admit it as regards thought. Again, as regards beauty, the man who fails to see its incomparable excellence in this respect merely shows his own deficiency in the appreciation of all that is noblest in man. True or not true, the entire Story of the Cross, from its commencement in prophetic aspiration to its culmination in the Gospel, is by far the most magnificent [presentation] in literature. And surely the fact of its having all been lived does not detract from its poetic value. Nor does the fact of its being capable of appropriation by the individual Christian of to-day as still a vital religion detract from its sublimity. Only to a man wholly destitute of spiritual perception can it be that Christianity should fail to appear the greatest exhibition of the beautiful, the sublime, and of all else that appeals to our spiritual nature, which has ever been known upon our earth.

Yet this side of its adaptation is turned only towards men of highest culture. The most remarkable thing about Christianity is its adaptation to all sorts and conditions of men. Are you highly intellectual? There is in its problems, historical and philosophical, such worlds of material as you may spend your life upon with the same interminable interest as is open to the students of natural science. Or are you but a peasant in your parish church, with knowledge of little else than your Bible? Still are you ...[64]

Regeneration.

How remarkable is the doctrine of Regeneration *per se*, as it is stated in the New Testament[65], and how completely it fits in with the non-demonstrative character of Revelation to reason alone, with the hypothesis of moral probation, &c. Now this doctrine is one of the distinctive notes of

Christianity. That is, Christ foretold repeatedly and distinctly—as did also His apostles after Him—that while those who received the Holy Ghost, who came to the Father through faith in the Son, who were born again of the Spirit, (and many other synonymous phrases,) would be absolutely certain of Christian truth as it were by direct vision or intuition, the carnally minded on the other hand would not be affected by any amount of direct evidence, even though one rose from the dead—as indeed Christ shortly afterwards did, with fulfilment of this prediction. Thus scepticism may be taken by Christians as corroborating Christianity.

By all means let us retain our independence of judgement; but this is pre-eminently a matter in which pure agnostics must abstain from arrogance and consider the facts impartially as unquestionable phenomena of experience.

Shortly after the death of Christ, this phenomenon which had been foretold by Him occurred, and appears to have done so for the first time. It has certainly continued to manifest itself ever since, and has been attributed by professed historians to that particular moment in time called Pentecost, producing much popular excitement and a large number of Christian believers.

But, whether or not we accept this account, it is unquestionable that the apostles were filled with faith in the person and office of their Master, which is enough to justify His doctrine of regeneration.

Conversions.

St. Augustine after thirty years of age, and other Fathers, bear testimony to a sudden, enduring and extraordinary change in themselves, called *conversion*[66].

Now this experience has been repeated and testified to by countless millions of civilized men and women in all nations and all degrees of culture. It signifies not whether the conversion be sudden or gradual, though, as a psychological phenomenon, it is more remarkable when sudden and there is no symptom of mental aberration otherwise. But even as a gradual growth in mature age, its evidential value is not less. (Cf. Bunyan, &c.)

In all cases it is not a mere change of belief or opinion; this is by no means the point; the point is that it is a modification of character, more or less profound.

Seeing what a complex thing is character, this change therefore cannot be simple. That it may all be due to so-called natural causes is no evidence against its so-called supernatural source, unless we beg the whole question of the Divine in Nature. To pure agnostics the evidence from conversions and regeneration lies in the bulk of these psychological phenomena, shortly after the death of Christ, with their continuance ever since, their general similarity all over the world, &c., &c.

Christianity and Pain.

Christianity, from its foundation in Judaism, has throughout been a religion of sacrifice and sorrow. It has been a religion of blood and tears, and yet of profoundest happiness to its votaries. The apparent paradox is due to its depth, and to the union of these seemingly diverse roots in Love. It has been throughout and growingly a religion—or rather let us say *the* religion—of Love, with these apparently opposite qualities. Probably it is only those whose characters have been deepened by experiences gained in this religion itself who are so much as capable of intelligently resolving this paradox.

Fakirs hang on hooks, Pagans cut themselves and even their children, sacrifice captives, &c., for the sake of propitiating diabolical deities. The Jewish and Christian idea of sacrifice is doubtless a survival of this idea of God by way of natural causation, yet this is no evidence against the completed idea of the Godhead being [such as the Christian belief represents it], for supposing the completed idea to be true, the earlier ideals would have been due to the earlier inspirations, in accordance with the developmental method of Revelation hereafter to be discussed[67].

But Christianity, with its roots in Judaism, is, as I have said, *par excellence* the religion of sorrow, because it reaches to truer and deeper levels of our spiritual nature, and therefore has capabilities both of sorrow and joy which are presumably non-existent except in civilized man. I mean the sorrows and the joys of a fully evolved spiritual life—such as were attained wonderfully early, historically speaking, in the case of the Jews, and are now universally diffused throughout Christendom. In short, the sorrows and the joys in question are those which arise from the fully developed consciousness of sin against a God of Love, as distinguished from propitiation of malignant spirits. These joys and sorrows are wholly spiritual, not merely physical, and culminate in the cry,'Thou desirest no sacrifice.... The sacrifice of God is a troubled spirit[68].'

I agree with Pascal[69] that there is virtually nothing to be gained by being a theist as distinguished from a Christian. Unitarianism is only an affair of the reason—a merely abstract theory of the mind, having nothing to do with the heart, or the real needs of mankind. It is only when it takes the New Testament, tears out a few of its leaves relating to the divinity of Christ, and appropriates all the rest, that its system becomes in any degree possible as a basis for personal religion.

If there is a Deity it seems to be in some indefinite degree more probable that He should impart a Revelation than that He should not.

Women, as a class, are in all countries much more disposed to Christianity than men. I think the scientific explanation of this is to be found in the causes assigned in my essay on *Mental differences between Men and Women*[70]. But, if Christianity be supposed true, there would, of course, be a more ultimate explanation of a religious kind—as in all other cases where causation is concerned. And, in that case I have no doubt that the largest part of the explanation would consist in the passions of women being less ardent than those of men, and also much more kept under restraint by social conditions of life. This applies not only to purity, but likewise to most of the other psychological *differentiae* between the sexes, such as ambition, selfishness, pride of power, and so forth. In short, the whole ideal of Christian ethics is of a feminine as distinguished from a masculine type[71]. Now nothing is so inimical to Christian belief as un-Christian conduct. This is especially the case as regards impurity; for whether the fact be explained on religious or non-religious grounds, it has more to do with unbelief than has the speculative reason. Consequently, woman is, for all these reasons, the 'fitter' type for receiving and retaining Christian belief.

Modern agnosticism is performing this great service to Christian faith; it is silencing all rational scepticism of the *a priori* kind. And this it is bound to do more and more the purer it becomes. In every generation it must henceforth become more and more recognized by logical thinking, that all antecedent objections to Christianity founded on reason alone are *ipso facto* nugatory. Now, all the strongest objections to Christianity have ever been those of the antecedent kind; hence the effect of modern thinking is that of more and more diminishing the purely speculative difficulties, such as that of the Incarnation, &c. In other words the force of Butler's argument about our being incompetent judges[72] is being more and more increased.

And the logical development of this lies in the view already stated about natural causation. For, just as pure agnosticism must allow that reason is incompetent to adjudicate *a priori* for or against Christian miracles, including the Incarnation, so it must further allow that, if they ever took place, reason can have nothing to say against their being all of one piece with causation in general. Hence, so far as reason is concerned, pure agnosticism must allow that it is only the event which can ultimately prove whether Christianity is true or false. 'If it be of God we cannot overthrow it, lest haply we be found even to fight against God.' But the individual cannot wait for this empirical determination. What then is he to do? The unbiassed answer of pure agnosticism ought reasonably to be, in the words of John Hunter, 'Do not think; try.' That is, in this case, try the only experiment available—the experiment of faith. Do the doctrine, and if Christianity be true, the verification will come, not indeed mediately through any course of speculative reason, but immediately by spiritual intuition. Only if a man has faith enough to make this venture honestly, will he be in a just position for deciding the issue. Thus viewed it would seem that the experiment of faith is not a 'fool's experiment'; but, on the contrary, so that there is enough *prima facie* evidence to arrest serious attention, such an experimental trial would seem to be the rational duty of a pure agnostic.

It is a fact that Christian belief is much more due to doing than to thinking, as prognosticated by the New Testament. 'If any man will do His will, he shall know of the doctrine, whether it be of God' (St. John vii. 17). And surely, even on grounds of reason itself, it should be allowed that, supposing Christianity to be 'of God,' it *ought* to appeal to the spiritual rather than to the rational side of our nature.

Even within the region of pure reason (or the '*prima facie* case') modern science, as directed on the New Testament criticism, has surely done more for Christianity than against it. For, after half a century of battle over the text by the best scholars, the dates of the Gospels have been fixed within the first century, and at least four of St. Paul's epistles have had their authenticity proved beyond doubt. Now this is enough to destroy all eighteenth-century criticism as to the doubtfulness of the historical existence of Christ and His apostles, 'inventions of priests,' &c., which was the most formidable kind of criticism of all. There is no longer any question as to historical facts, save the miraculous, which, however, are ruled out by negative criticism on merely *a priori* grounds. This remaining—and, *ex hypothesi*, necessary—doubt is of very different importance from the other.

Again, the Pauline epistles of proved authenticity are enough for all that is wanted to show the belief of Christ's contemporaries.

These are facts of the first order of importance to have proved. Old Testament criticism is as yet too immature to consider.

Plan in Revelation.

The views which I entertained on this subject when an undergraduate [i.e. the ordinary orthodox views] were abandoned in presence of the theory of Evolution—i.e. the theory of natural causation as probably furnishing a scientific explanation [of the religious phenomena of Judaism] or, which is the same thing, an explanation in terms of ascertainable causes up to some certain point; which however in this particular case cannot be determined within wide limits, so that the history of Israel will always embody an element of 'mystery' much more than any other history.

It was not until twenty-five years later that I saw clearly the full implications of my present views on natural causation. As applied to this particular case these views show that to a theist, at all events (i.e. to any one who on independent grounds has accepted the theory of Theism), it ought not to make much difference to the evidential value of the Divine Plan of Revelation as exhibited in the Old and New Testaments, even if it be granted that the whole has been due to so-called natural causes only. I say, 'not much difference,' for that it ought to make some difference I do not deny. Take a precisely analogous case. The theory of evolution by natural causes is often said to make no logical difference in the evidence of plan or design manifested in organic nature—it being only a question of *modus operandi* whether all pieces of organic machinery were produced suddenly or by degrees; the evidence of design is equally there in either case. Now I have shown elsewhere that this is wrong[73]. It may not make much difference to a man who is already a theist, for then it is but a question of *modus*, but it makes a great difference to the evidence of Theism.

So it is in evidence of plan in proof of a revelation. If there had been no alleged revelation up to the present time, and if Christ were now to appear suddenly in His first advent in all the power and glory which Christians expect for His second, the proof of His revelation would be demonstrative. So that, as a mere matter of evidence, a sudden revelation might be much more convincing than a gradual one. But it would be quite out of analogy with causation in nature[74]. Besides, even a gradual revelation might be given easily, which would be of demonstrative value—as by making prophecies of historical events, scientific discoveries, &c., so clear as to be unmistakeable. But, as before shown, a demonstrative revelation has not been made, and there may well be good reasons why it should not. Now, if there are such reasons (e.g. our state of probation), we can well see that the gradual unfolding of a plan of revelation, from earliest dawn of history to the end of the world ('I speak as a fool') is much preferable to a sudden manifestation sufficiently late in the world's history to be historically attested for all subsequent time. For

> 1st. Gradual evolution is in analogy with God's other work.
>
> 2nd. It does not leave Him without witness at any time during the historical period.
>
> 3rd. It gives ample scope for persevering research at all times—i.e. a moral test, and not merely an intellectual assent to some one *(ex hypothesi)* unequivocally attested event in history.

The *appearance* of plan in revelation is, in fact, certainly remarkable enough to arrest serious attention.

If revelation has been of a progressive character, then it follows that it must have been so, not only historically, but likewise intellectually, morally, and spiritually. For thus only could it be always adapted to the advancing conditions of the human race. This reflection destroys all those numerous objections against Scripture on account of the absurdity or immorality of its statements or precepts, unless it can be shown that the modifications suggested by criticism as requisite to bring the statements or precepts into harmony with modern advancement would have been as well adapted to the requirements of the world at the date in question, as were the actual statements or precepts before us.

Supposing Christianity true, it is certain that the revelation which it conveys has been predetermined at least since the dawn of the historical period. This is certain because the objective evidences of Christianity as a revelation have their origin in that dawn. And these objective evidences are throughout [evidence] of a scheme, in which the end can be seen from the beginning. And the very methods whereby this scheme is itself revealed are such (still supposing that it is a scheme) as present remarkable evidences of design. These methods are, broadly speaking, miracles, prophecy and the results of the teaching, &c., upon mankind. Now one may show that no better methods could conceivably have been designed for the purpose of latter-day evidence, combined with moral and religious teaching throughout. The mere fact of it being so largely incorporated with secular history renders the Christian religion unique: so to speak, the world, throughout its entire historical period, has been constituted the canvas on which this divine revelation has been painted—and painted so gradually that not until the process had been going on for a couple of thousand years was it possible to perceive the subject thereof.

Christian Dogmas.

Whether or not Christ was Himself divine would make no difference so far as the consideration of Christianity as the highest phase of evolution is concerned, or from the purely secular [scientific] point of view. From the religious point of view, or that touching the relation of God to man, it would of course make a great difference; but the difference belongs to the same region of thought as that which applies to all the previous moments of evolution. Thus the passage from the non-moral to the moral appears, from the secular or scientific point of view, to be due, as far as we can see, to mechanical causes in natural selection or what not. But, just as in the case of the passage from the non-mental to the mental, &c., this passage may have been *ultimately* due to divine volition, and *must have been so due* on the theory of Theism. Therefore, I say, it makes no difference from a secular or scientific point of view whether or not Christ was Himself divine; since, in either case, the movement which He inaugurated was the proximate or phenomenal cause of the observable results.

Thus, even the question of the divinity of Christ ultimately resolves itself into the question of all questions—viz. is or is not mechanical causation 'the outward and visible form of an inward and spiritual grace'? Is it phenomenal or ontological; ultimate or derivative?

Similarly as regards the redemption. Whether or not Christ was really divine, in as far as a belief in His divinity has been a necessary cause of the moral and religious evolution which has resulted from His life on earth, it has equally and so far 'saved His people from their sins'; that is, of course, it has saved them from their own sense of sin as an abiding curse. Whether or not He has effected any corresponding change of an objective character in the ontological sphere, again depends on the 'question of questions' just stated.

Reasonableness of the Doctrines of the Incarnation and the Trinity.

Pure agnostics and those who search for God in Christianity should have nothing to do with metaphysical theology. *That* is a department of enquiry which, *ex hypothesi*, is transcendental, and is only to be considered after Christianity has been accepted. The doctrines of the Incarnation and the Trinity seemed to me most absurd in my agnostic days. But now, as a *pure* agnostic, I see in them no rational difficulty at all. As to the Trinity, the plurality of persons is necessarily implied in the companion doctrine of the Incarnation. So that at best there is here but one difficulty, since, duality being postulated in the doctrine of the Incarnation, there is no further difficulty for pure agnosticism in the doctrine of plurality. Now at one time it seemed to me impossible that any proposition, verbally intelligible as such, could be more violently absurd than that of the doctrine [of the Incarnation]. Now I see that this standpoint is wholly irrational, due only to the blindness of reason itself promoted by [purely] scientific habits of thought. 'But it is opposed to common sense.' No doubt, utterly so; but so it *ought* to be if true. Common sense is merely a [rough] register of common experience; but the Incarnation, if it ever took place, whatever else it may have been, at all events cannot have been a common event. 'But it is derogatory to God to become man.' How do you know? Besides, Christ was not an ordinary man. Both negative criticism and the historical effects of His life prove this; while, if we for a moment adopt the Christian point of view for the sake of argument, the whole *raison d'être* of mankind is bound up in Him. Lastly, there are considerations *per contra*, rendering an incarnation antecedently probable[75]. On antecedent grounds there *must* be mysteries unintelligible to reason as to the nature of God, &c., supposing a revelation to be made at all. Therefore their occurrence in Christianity *is* no proper objection to Christianity. Why, again, stumble *a priori* over the doctrine of the Trinity—especially as man himself is a triune being, of body, mind (i.e. reason), and spirit (i.e. moral, aesthetic, religious faculties)? The unquestionable union of these no less unquestionably distinct orders of being in man is known immediately as a fact of experience, but is as unintelligible by any process of logic or reason as is the alleged triunity of God.

Adam, the Fall, the Origin of Evil.

These, all taken together as Christian dogmas, are undoubtedly hard hit by the scientific proof of evolution (but are the *only* dogmas which can fairly be said to be so), and, as constituting the logical basis of the whole plan, they certainly do appear at first sight necessarily to involve in their destruction that of the entire superstructure. But the question is whether, after all, they have been destroyed for a pure agnostic. In other words, whether my principles are not as applicable in turning the flank of infidelity here as everywhere else.

First, as regards Adam and Eve, observe, to begin with, that long before Darwin the story of man in Paradise was recognized by thoughtful theologians as allegorical. Indeed, read with unprejudiced eyes, the first chapters of Genesis ought always to have been seen to be a poem as distinguished from a history: nor could it ever have been mistaken for a history, but for preconceived ideas on the matter of inspiration. But to pure agnostics there should be no such preconceived ideas; so that nowadays no presumption should be raised against it as inspired, merely because it has been proved not to be a history—and this even though we cannot see of what it is allegorical. For, supposing it inspired, it has certainly done good service in the past and can do so likewise in the present, by giving an allegorical, though not a literal, starting-point for the Divine Plan of Redemption.

The evidence of Natural and Revealed Religion compared.

It is often said that evolution of organic forms gives as good evidence of design as would their special creation, inasmuch as all the facts of adaptation, in which the evidence consists, are there in either case. But here it is overlooked that the very question at issue is thus begged. The question is, Are these facts of adaptation *per se* sufficient evidence of design as their cause? But if it be allowed, as it must be, that under hypothesis of evolution by natural causes the facts of adaptation belong to the same category as all the other facts of nature, no more special argument for design can be founded on these facts than on any others in nature. So that the facts of adaptation, like all other facts, are only available as arguments for design when it is assumed that all natural causation is of a mental character: which assumption merely begs the question of design anywhere. Or, in other words, on the supposition of their having been due to natural causes, the facts of adaptation are only then available as *per se* good evidence of design, when it has already been assumed that, *qua* due to natural causes, they are due to design.

Natural religion resembles Revealed religion in this. Supposing both divine, both have been arranged so that, as far as reason can lead us, there is only enough evidence of design to arouse serious attention to the question of it. In other words, as regards both, the attitude of pure reason ought to be that of pure agnosticism. (Observe that the inadequacy of teleology, or design in nature, to prove Theism has been expressly recognized by all the more intellectual Christians of all ages, although such recognition has become more general since Darwin. On this point I may refer to Pascal especially[76], and many other authors.) This is another striking analogy between Nature and Revelation, supposing both to have emanated from the same author—i.e. quite as much so as identity of developmental method in both.

Supposing the hypothesis of design in both to be true, it follows that in both this hypothesis can be alike verified only by the organ of immediate intuition—i.e. that other mode of human apprehension which is supplementary to the rational. Here again we note the analogy. And if a man has this supplementary mode of apprehending the highest truth (by hypothesis such), it will be his duty to exercise his spiritual eyesight in searching for God in nature as in revelation, when (still on our present hypothesis that 'God is, and is the rewarder of them who seek Him diligently') he will find that his subjective evidence of God in Nature and in Revelation will mutually corroborate one another—so yielding additional evidence to his reason.

The teleology of Revelation supplements that of Nature, and so, to the spiritually minded man, they logically and mutually corroborate one another.

Paley's writings form an excellent illustration of the identity of the teleological argument from Nature and from Revelation; though a very imperfect illustration of the latter taken by itself, inasmuch as he treats only of the New Testament, and even of that very partially—ignoring all that went before Christ, and much of what happened after the apostles. Yet Paley himself does not seem to have observed the similarity of the argument, as developed in his *Natural Theology* and *Evidences of Christianity* respectively. But no one has developed the argument better in both cases. His great defect was in not perceiving that this teleological argument, *per se*, is not in either case enough to convince, but only to arouse serious attention. Paley everywhere represents that such an appeal to reason alone ought to be sufficient. He fails to see that if it were, there could be no room for faith. In other words, he fails to recognize the spiritual organ in man, and its complementary object, grace in God. So far he fails to be a Christian. And, whether Theism and Christianity be true or false, it is certain that the teleological argument alone *ought* to result, not in conviction, but in agnosticism.

The antecedent improbability against a miracle being wrought by a man without a moral object is apt to be confused with that of its being done by

God with an adequate moral object. The former is immeasurably great; the latter is only equal to that of the theory of Theism—i.e. *nil.*

Christian Demonology[77].

It will be said, 'However you may seek to explain away *a priori* objections to miracles on *a priori* grounds, there remains the fact that Christ accepted the current superstition in regard to diabolic possession. Now the devils damn the doctrine. For you must choose the horn of your dilemma, either the current theory was true or it was not. If you say true, you must allow that the same theory is true for all similar stages of culture, [but not for the later stages,] and therefore that the most successful exorcist is Science, albeit Science works not by faith in the theory, but by rejection of it. Observe, the diseases are so well described by the record, that there is no possibility of mistaking them. Hence you must suppose that they were due to devils in A.D. 30, and to nervous disorders in A.D. 1894. On the other hand, if you choose the other horn, you must accept either the hypothesis of the ignorance or that of the mendacity of Christ.'

The answer is, that either hypothesis may be accepted by Christianity. For the sake of argument we may exclude the question whether the acceptance of the devil theory by Christ was really historical, or merely attributed to Him by His biographers after His death. If Christ knew that the facts were not due to devils, He may also have known it was best to fall in with current theory, rather than to puzzle the people with a lecture on pathology. If He did not know, why should He, if He had previously 'emptied Himself' of omniscience? In either case, if He had denied the current theory, He would have been giving evidence of scientific knowledge or of scientific intuition beyond the culture of His time, and this, as in countless other cases, was not in accordance with His method, which, whether we suppose it divine or human, has nowhere proved His divine mission by foreknowledge of natural science.

The particular question of Christ and demonology is but part of a much larger one.

Darwin's Difficulty[78].

The answer to Darwin's objection about so small a proportion of mankind having ever heard of Christ, is manifold:—

1. Supposing Christianity true, it is the highest and final revelation; i.e. the scheme of revelation has been developmental. Therefore, it follows from the very method that the larger proportion of mankind should never hear of Christ, i.e. all who live before His advent.

2. But these were not left 'without witness.' They all had their religion and their moral sense, each at its appropriate stage of development. Therefore 'the times of ignorance God winked at' (Acts xvii. 30).

3. Moreover these men were not devoid of benefit from Christ, because it is represented that He died for all men—i.e. but for Him [i.e. apart from the knowledge of what was to come] God would not have 'winked at the times of ignorance.' The efficacy of atonement is represented as transcendental, and not dependent on the accident of hearing about the Atoner.

4. It is remarkable that of all men Darwin should have been worsted by this fallacious argument. For it has received its death-blow from the theory of evolution: i.e. if it be true that evolution has been the method of natural causation, and if it be true that the method of natural causation is due to a Divinity, then it follows that the lateness of Christ's appearance on earth must have been designed. For it is certain that He could not have appeared at any earlier date without having violated the method of evolution. Therefore, on the theory of Theism, He *ought* to have appeared when He did—i.e. at the earliest possible moment in history.

So as to the suitability of the moment of Christ's appearance in other respects. Even secular historians are agreed as to the suitability of the combinations, and deduce the success of His system of morals and religion from this fact. So with students of comparative religions.

FOOTNOTES:

[59] [I.e. a theory which comes at first as a shock to the current teaching of Christianity, but is finally seen to be in no antagonism to its necessary principles.—ED.]

[60] [I.e. the battle in regard to the Christian texts or documents.—ED.]

[61] See Gore's *Bampton Lectures*, pp. 74 ff.

[62] Matt, xxviii. 17; Acts ii. 13.

[63] *Three Essays on Theism*, p. 255.

[64] [Note unfinished.—ED.]

[65] [George Romanes began to make a collection of N.T. texts bearing on the subject.—ED.]

[66] See Pascal, *Pensées*, p. 245.

[67] [The notes on this subject were often too fragmentary for publication.—ED.]

[68] Ps. li.

[69] *Pensées*, pp. 91-93.

[70] See *Nineteenth Century*, May 1887.

[71] [The essay mentioned above should be read in explanation of this expression. George Romanes' meaning would be more accurately expressed, I think, had he said: 'The ideal of Christian character holds in prominence the elements which we regard as characteristically feminine, e.g. development of affections, readiness of trust, love of service, readiness to suffer, &c.'—ED.]

[72] See *Analogy*, part i. ch. 7; part ii. ch. 3, 4, &c.

[73] See Conclusion of *Darwin and After Darwin*, part I.

[74] I should somewhere show how much better a treatise Butler might have written had he known about evolution as the general law of nature.

[75] See Gore's *Bampton Lectures*, lect. ii.

[76] *Pensées*, pp. 205 ff.

[77] [Romanes' line of argument in this note seems to me impossible to maintain. The emphasis which Jesus Christ lays on diabolic agency is so great that, if it is not a reality, He must be regarded either as seriously misled about realities which concern the spiritual life, or else as seriously misleading others. And in neither case could He be even the perfect Prophet. I think I am justified in explaining my disagreement with Romanes' argument at this point particularly.—ED.]

[78] [There is nothing in Darwin's *writings* which seems to me to justify Romanes in attributing this difficulty to him specially. But he knew Darwin so intimately and reverenced him so profoundly that he is not likely to have been in error on the subject.—ED.]

CONCLUDING NOTE BY THE EDITOR:—

The intellectual attitude towards Christianity expressed in these notes may be described as—(1) 'pure agnosticism' in the region of the scientific 'reason,' coupled with (2) a vivid recognition of the spiritual necessity of faith and of the legitimacy and value of its intuitions; (3) a perception of the positive strength of the historical and spiritual evidences of Christianity.

George Romanes came to recognize, as in these written notes so also in conversation, that it was 'reasonable to be a Christian believer' before the activity or habit of faith had been recovered. His life was cut short very soon after this point was reached; but it will surprise no one to learn that the writer of these 'Thoughts' returned before his death to that full, deliberate communion with the Church of Jesus Christ which he had for so many years been conscientiously compelled to forego. In his case the 'pure in heart' was after a long period of darkness allowed, in a measure before his death, to 'see God.'

Fecisti nos ad te, Domine; et inquietum est cor nostrum donec requiescat in te.

C.G.

Milton Keynes UK
Ingram Content Group UK Ltd.
UKHW031049120324
439302UK00006B/467